Costa Brava

D1393160

COLLINS

Glasgow & London

First published 1990
Copyright © William Collins Sons & Company Limited
Printed and Published by
William Collins Sons & Company Limited
ISBN 0 00 435773-6

HOW TO USE THIS BOOK

Your Collins Traveller Guide will help you find your way around your chosen destination quickly and easily. It is colour-coded for easy reference:

The blue-coded 'topic' section answers the question 'I would like to see or do something; where do I go and what do I see when I get there?' A simple, clear layout provides an alphabetical list of activities and events, offers you a selection of each, tells you how to get there, what it will cost, when it is open and what to expect. Each topic in the list has its own simplified map, showing the position of each item and the nearest landmark or transport access, for instant orientation. Whether your interest is Architecture or Sport you can find all the information you need quickly and simply. Where major resorts within an area require in-depth treatment, they follow the main topics section in alphabetical order.

The red-coded section is a lively and informative gazetteer. In one alphabetical list you can find essential facts about the main places and cultural items - 'What is La Bastille?', 'Who was Michelangelo?' - as well as practical and invaluable travel information. It covers everything you need to know to help you enjoy yourself and get the most out of your time away, from Accommodation through Babysitters, Car Hire, Food, Health, Money, Newspapers, Taxis and Telephones to Zoos.

Cross-references: Type in small capitals - CHURCHES - tells you that more information on an item is available within the topic on churches. A-Z in bold - A-Z - tells you that more information is available on an item within the gazetteer. Simply look under the appropriate heading. A name in bold - **Holy Cathedral** - also tells you that more information on an item is available in the gazetteer under that particular heading.

Packed full of information and easy to use - you'll always know where you are with your Collins Traveller Guide!

Photographs by **Phil Springthorpe**

INTRODUCTION

Catalunya, in the north-east corner of the Iberian Peninsula, is the wealthiest of Spain's 17 autonomous regions and Girona is one of Catalunya's four provinces. Along the varied coastline of the Costa Brava lies the province's famous summer holiday playground. Lesser known is Girona city, its enchanting capital, and the interior of woodland, lush meadow and good farmland cut through by fast streams and full-flowing rivers. Picturesque farmhouses and villages, and impressive monasteries and churches, all built of honey-coloured stone, lie scattered among beautiful landscapes. The modest appearance or unpromising outskirts of some busy commercial towns belie their charm and attractions. The high peaks and verdant valleys of the Pyrenees form a spectacular and protective backdrop.

Forget images of Spain like fiery flamenco dancers or stark castles on scorched and empty plains. This is green and productive Catalan country with its separate language and cultural traditions. Here the genteel *sardana* is danced and fine examples of Romanesque, Gothic and Modernist architecture are jewels in its rich artistic heritage.

Since people began moving between the rest of Europe and Iberia, this part of the peninsula has been on the main route. A street which is still at the heart of old Girona city was part of Rome's great Via Augusta. Conquering or retreating armies have always passed this way. Through here European religious and cultural influence came creeping into Spain. Over the centuries Catalans benefited economically and socially from being more open to the ways of foreigners than their Spanish cousins. When they were repressed from Madrid by centralist Spain's kings and dictators, their language and culture gave them strength and hope. Gironins proudly claim their province as the fountainhead of the Catalan nation. The *sardana* originated here and its circle of dancers gently stepping in unison is said to depict the Catalan people's unity.

Large-scale foreign tourism to the Mediterranean started on the Costa Brava, which is so easily accessible for many Europeans. Now this is the most heavily urbanized of Spain's coastlines. But it has not been devastated by development as some commentators bewail. Parts are untouched or have little development, much of the rest has villas in extensive but attractive urbanizations, and high-rises are restricted to some resort towns. As elsewhere, there have been errors of bad plan-

ning but new laws and environmental awareness should prevent their repetition. By worldwide comparison, the standard of the Costa Brava's tourism infrastructure rates highly.

Over 90 official beaches, mostly clean and coarse sand, present a choice from wide, long stretches to small, cosy coves (*calas*). Many are backed by pine woods which offer welcome shade. Resorts vary from big, brash Lloret de Mar and Platja d'Aro to quieter, prettier Tossa de Mar and Cadaqués, and tiny, more laid-back Tamariu and Sa Riera. Towns like Blanes, Palamós and Roses welcome many summer visitors but off-season revert to their primary roles as commercial centres and fishing ports. Accommodation choices range from many camp sites, simple *hostals*, apartments, villas and converted farmhouses to hotels of every grade. It is a media myth that the Costa Brava is entirely package holiday hotel territory.

As with type of resort and places to stay, so it is with places to eat and nightlife. Be it very low-budget rough and tumble, high-cost luxury and elegance or something in between you want on holiday, it's very much a case of you make your choice and you take your pick. Opportunities to enjoy a favourite sport, or try a different one, are equally varied and numerous. To name a few, there are sailing, windsurfing, diving, tennis, riding and golf. Boat excursions between resorts or beaches, walks along coastal paths and visits to local sights, markets, museums and cultural centres are among other things to do. And there is always the temptation to browse and buy in the many *artesanías*, art galleries, boutiques and other interesting shops.

One of the *sardanas* tells of a shepherd's love for a mermaid, a marriage of land and sea. Its theme is taken up in the newly-coined name of Costa Brava Girona to hint that, beyond the beach resorts, there's a great deal more to see and do in the province of Girona at any time of the year. As you will see in this guide, the province presents a sightseeing treasure trove: ancient stones like the Greek and Roman ruins of Empúries; exceptional buildings like the monastery of Ripoll; colourful gardens like Marimurtra; nature parks like the Zona Volcànica de la Garrotxa; fascinating museums like that of Salvador Dalí in Figueres; and beguiling medieval villages like Besalú.

Take almost any road and you will come across stunning landscapes, picturesque villages and, often, a gem of Romanesque architecture. There are inland resorts too, like the health spa of Caldes de Malavella, the quiet towns of Les Guilleries and the four Pyrenean winter sports centres. Banyoles lake is a premier venue for rowing events. Wooded mountain areas beckon hikers and climbers, and well-stocked rivers draw fishing enthusiasts.

If that is not enough to entice you to discover the interior of the province, there is also Girona city, small but packed with charm and interest. Its old part, encircled by walls and rising above the Riu Onyar, is a compact maze of stairways, cobbled streets and pretty *plaças* with grand and modest buildings in different architectural styles. Good museums and active cultural centres, interesting art galleries and shops, lively open-air cafés and a wide choice of eating places add to the city's attraction. Students huddled in earnest discussion, people on *paseo* and entranced tourists add to its animation. During any season it is a very seductive place.

Among the Catalans there is a great enthusiasm for the arts. Although Girona is the centre of the cultural life of the province, many of the coastal and inland towns maintain their own cultural centres and present summer festivals of music and dance. Some are of the highest standard and offer an added dimension for holiday pleasure. Summer is also the season for most of the fiestas which are celebrated with much colour, noise and gaiety, not to mention eating and drinking, for the Catalans are also very enthusiastic about good food and drink.

The gastronomic tradition is especially strong in Girona province and

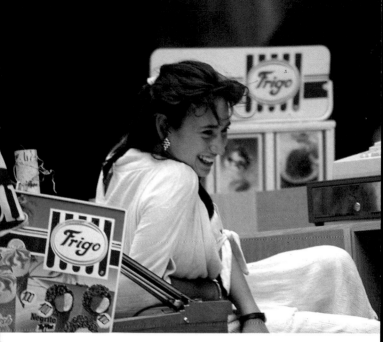

there are distinct variations between its different parts. In the resorts, a lot of eating places, including some hotel dining rooms, serve cheap and nasty stomach fillers. You'll be glad if you avoid them because there are many more delightful and welcoming places, for every budget, where traditional dishes or their lighter, modern style derivatives are prepared with great care and pride.

Whether your taste is for food or fun the Costa Brava can accommodate you. So relax and soak up the atmosphere or go out and get caught up in the excitement of this premier holiday area. But whatever you do enjoy yourself!

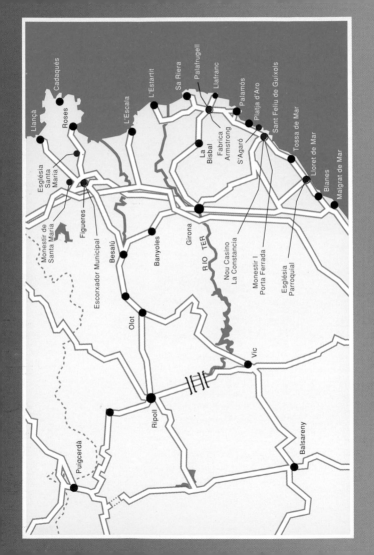

ESGLÉSIA PARROQUIAL Pl de L'Església, Lloret de Mar.
• 1000-1200, 1800-2000.
This late Gothic church of Sant Romà has an added Modernist chapel and a distinctive cupola decorated with multi-coloured ceramic tiles.

MONESTIR I PORTA FERRADA Pl de Monestir,
Sant Feliu de Guíxols.
The ruined monastery buildings include the Porta Ferrada, a decorative 11thC facade, and a Baroque portal, the Arc de Sant Benet. See **MUSEUMS 1**.

NOU CASINO LA CONSTANCIA Psg de Guíxols,
Sant Feliu de Guíxols.
Influenced by the Mudéjar style (see **A-Z**), *and finished in 1903. This is one of several Modernist buildings in the town.*

S'AGARÓ 2 km north of Sant Feliu de Guíxols.
This exclusive residential development, begun by the Ensesas family in the 1920s, shows late Modernist influence in many of its villas. See **A-Z**.

FABRICA ARMSTRONG Palafrugell.
This cork factory (1900-4) has fine wrought-iron details and an unusual metal tower. Other buildings in the town also show Modernist style.

ESGLÉSIA SANTA MARIA Castelló d'Empúries.
A 13thC building with an impressive portal and a 15thC carved alabaster altarpiece.

ESCORXADOR MUNICIPAL Pl de l'Escorxador, Figueres.
Municipal cultural centre. Built in 1903 as a slaughterhouse in Modernist style by Josep Azemar, whose other buildings in the town include Casa Cusí (1894) and Casa Salleras (1910).

MONESTIR DE SANTA MARIA Vilabertran.
2 km north of Figueres.
A Romanesque (see **A-Z**) *church with tower, cloister and monastery cells with Gothic additions. Well worth a visit. See* **EXCURSION 1**.

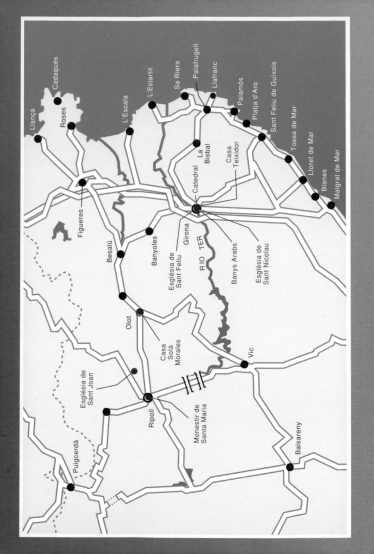

CASA SOLÀ MORALES Firal, Olot.
Rebuilt (1915-16) by one of the leading Modernist architects, Domènech i Montaner, with sculptures by Eusebi Arnau.

MONESTIR DE SANTA MARIA Ripoll.
•0900-1300 & 1500-1900. Closed Mon. pm.
Parts of its cloister and portal with detailed carvings of biblical scenes survive from this monastery famed for its medieval scholarship. The folklore museum (see MUSEUMS 2) is worth a visit. See Santa Maria de Ripoll.

ESGLÉSIA DE SANT JOAN Sant Joan de les Abadesses.
•1000-1300, 1600-1900 daily (summer); Sat. & Sun. only (winter).
French influence is evident in this 12thC church. The high altar features remarkable polychrome carvings depicting the Descent from the Cross.

CATEDRAL Pl de la Catedral, Ciutat Vella, Girona.
•1000-1300, 1530-1930 Tues.-Sat. (summer); 1000-1300 Sat. and hol. only (winter).
Huge Gothic church with beautiful Romanesque (see A-Z) cloisters, and an interesting museum (see MUSEUMS 2). See EXCURSION 3, WALK 1, A-Z.

ESGLÉSIA DE SANT FELIU Pl Sant Feliu, Ciutat Vella, Girona.
•Opening times vary.
A fascinating mixture of Romanesque (see A-Z), Gothic and Baroque styles. See EXCURSION 3, WALK 1.

BANYS ARABS Ferran el Catòlic, Ciutat Vella, Girona.
•1000-1300 & 1630-1900 Tues.-Sun. Closed Sun. and hol. pm.
Late Romanesque (see A-Z) Arab baths. See EXCURSION 3, WALK 1.

ESGLÉSIA DE SANT NICOLAU Galligans, Ciutat Vella, Girona.
Small and well-proportioned church. See EXCURSION 3, WALK 1.

CASA TEIXIDOR Santa Eugènia, Girona.
Built in the Eixample between 1918-22 by the town's leading Modernist architect, Rafael Masó. Nearby is his Farinera Teixidor (flour mill).

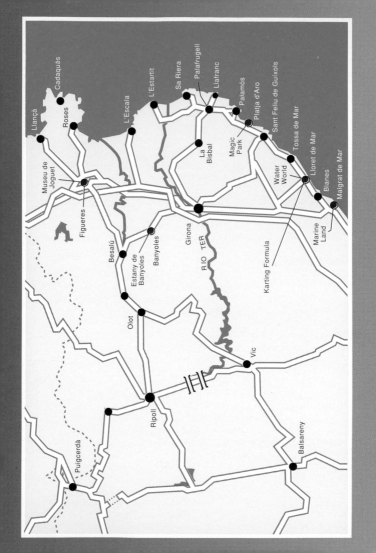

WATER WORLD Ctra Vidreres, Lloret de Mar.
- From 1000 daily May-Oct. Free bus from Lloret.

Exciting swimming pool and leisure complex with a wave machine, water slide, rapid river, mini golf, restaurants and other amenities.

MARINE LAND Malgrat de Mar.
- Dolphin and sea lion shows at 1030, 1230, 1530 & 1900 daily.

Aquarium and leisure centre popular for its dolphin and sea lion displays. There is also a small zoo, playground, restaurant and other facilities.

KARTING FORMULA Near Water World, Lloret de Mar.
- May-Oct.

Small circuit, go-karts to rent for children and adults. Similar facilities in Blanes, Santa Cristina d'Aro, Palamós, Palafrugell, L'Estartit and L'Escala.

MAGIC PARK Ctra Sant Feliu, Platja d'Aro.
- June-Sept.

Small-scale amusements and leisure centre.

MUSEU DE JOGUET Rambla 10, Figueres.
- 1000-1230, 1600-2000 Tues.-Sun.

A delightful private collection featuring some 3000 toys from the19th and 20thCs. See EXCURSION 1.

ESTANY DE BANYOLES Banyoles.

Escape from the hot beaches to this shaded lake side, ideal for swimming, boating and picnics. See EXCURSION 1.

DONKEY SAFARI
- May-Oct. afternoons. Contact local tourist offices for details.

Great fun for the young and not so young!

HORSE RIDING
- May-Oct. afternoons. Equestrian centres in various resorts.

Exciting excursions into the scenic countryside with halts for picnics and games. See SPORTS, A-Z.

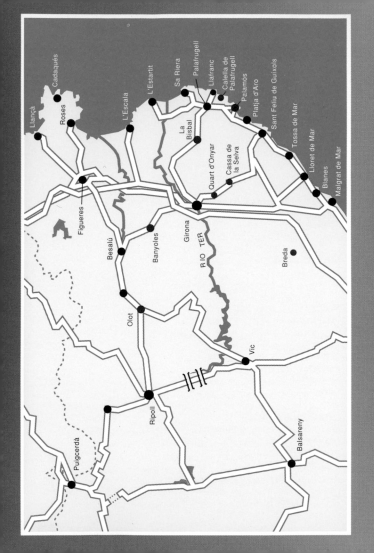

LA BISBAL 27 km east of Girona.
Decorative pottery at reasonable prices is available in this town's L'Aigüeta quarter. Juan Betrán, on the road to Palamós (see RESORTS 1, A-Z), also has a wide selection. The village of Pals (see TOWNS & VILLAGES 1, A-Z) has more good shops with some innovative designs. See TOWNS & VILLAGES 1, A-Z.

QUART D'ONYAR 7 km south of Girona.
A district producing black and green glazed pottery.

BREDA Serra de Montseny, 50 km north east of Barcelona.
This village produces good-quality domestic pottery for everyday use.

CASSA DE LA SELVA 13 km south east of Girona.
A good place to buy souvenirs and useful cork items.

BANYOLES 20 km north of Girona.
Has a long tradition of shoemaking, so explore its shops for something different for your feet. See EXCURSION 1, TOWNS & VILLAGES 2.

OLOT 60 km north west of Girona.
Religious carvings are the town's speciality. Begin in the shop of F. Cañados, Hostal del Sol 25. See TOWNS & VILLAGES 3.

OLOT 60 km north west of Girona.
On the second Sunday in July is the Aplec de la Sardan, a large gathering of groups from all over Catalunya (see A-Z) who dance their versions of the sardana (see A-Z). Visitors often get the chance to watch or join in the national dance in many other towns and villages. See TOWNS & VILLAGES 3.

CALELLA DE PALAFRUGELL 4 km south east of Palafrugell.
One of the best resorts in which to hear l'Havanera singers (see A-Z) perform sea shanties. See RESORTS 2.

PALAMÓS 49 km east of Girona.
In August the town hosts the Festival de la Cançó Marinera. Traditional sailors' songs are performed by the region's top singers. See RESORTS 1, A-Z.

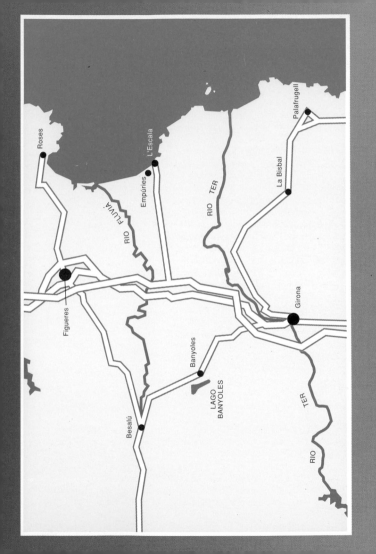

BANYOLES 20 km north of Girona.
A charming and historic town on the shores of a lake (see **CHILDREN**).
Notable sights include: the Museu Arqueològic Comarcal (see **MUSEUMS 2**)
*containing artefacts unearthed locally; the church of St Esteve, originally
built in the 9thC; and the scenic lake, the largest in Catalunya (see* **A-Z**),
which will be the site of events in the 1992 Barcelona Olympics (see **A-Z**).
*It offers numerous facilities for water sports, camping and picnics. Nearby is
the small village of Porqueres whose church has an interesting Romanesque
(see* **A-Z**) *portal. See* **CRAFTS & CUSTOMS**, **TOWNS & VILLAGES 2**.

BESALÚ 14 km north west of Banyoles.
*Medieval town boasting various attractions including: the Church of Sant
Pere, an outstanding example of Catalan Romanesque (see* **A-Z**); *the ruins of
the Church of Santa Maria, another Romanesque design; and the Church of
Sant Vicenç, which dates from the 12thC and has notable Lombard arches
and a rose window. The bridge over the River Fluvià also dates from the
Middle Ages; and unique in Spain, and one of only three in Europe, is the
mikwà, a Jewish ritual bath from the 12thC discovered in 1964 and since
restored. See* **HISTORIC SITES**, **TOWNS & VILLAGES 2**, **A-Z**.

FIGUERES 35 km north of Girona.
Site of the immensely popular Teatre-Museu Dalí (see **MUSEUMS 1**). *In the
Ramblas (shaded boulevard) in the centre of the town is the Museu de
l'Empordà (see* **MUSEUMS 1**), *containing exhibits illustrating the history of
Catalunya (see* **A-Z**). *Also worth visiting is the toy collection in the Museu
de Joguet (see* **CHILDREN**). *2 km north of the town is the beautiful
Romanesque (see* **A-Z**) *church of Vilabertran (see* **BUILDINGS 1**), *site of an
international music festival (see* **Events**). *See* **TOWNS & VILLAGES 2**, **A-Z**.

EMPÚRIES Sant Martí de Empúries, 56 km north east of Girona.
*The remains of a 6thC BC Greek settlement and later Roman town called
Emporiae. Roman troops landed here in 218 BC under the command of
Scipio the Elder during the campaign against Carthage. 2 km south is the
small fishing village and popular resort of L'Escala (see* **RESORTS 3**, **A-Z**),
*which has a variety of seafood restaurants, ideal for lunch after a morning
visiting the ancient ruins. See* **HISTORIC SITES**, **A-Z**.

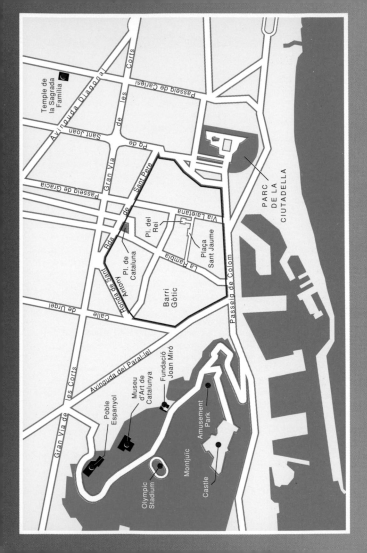

Barcelona

*1 day. Barcelona is 100 km from Girona; you can either take the A 11
motorway or the coastal route following the N II. There is also a regular
train service from Girona to Barcelona.*

Barcelona is the capital of Catalunya *(see **A-Z**)* and Spain's second
largest city. During its medieval golden age, the city reigned as queen
among Mediterranean ports. With an unmatched verve it is striving to
do so again: *Barcelona, Més Que Mai* (Barcelona, More than Ever) ban-
ners everywhere proclaim. As venue for the Summer Olympics of 1992
(see **A-Z**), the city is assured of world attention and it is in a ferment of
anticipation and preparation.

The city scores high in all areas of tourist interest. The Barri Gòtic
(Gothic quarter) built upon Roman Barcino, is a maze of alleys lined
with civic and residential buildings dating from the 13th 15thCs. The
Cathedral (or La Seu) has notable rose windows, a choir with carved
stalls and marble screen and a lovely cloister. Plaça del Rei exhibits a
beautiful assembly of Gothic buildings. The adjoining Museu d'Història
de la Ciutat (0900-1400, 1530-2030 Tues.-Sat.; 0900-1400 Sun.) is well
worth a visit, as is the Museu Frederic Marés with its rich sculpture collection (0900-1400, 1600-1900 Tues.-Sat.; 0900-1400 Sun.). Two grand
buildings dominate the Plaça Sant Jaume, the heart of the old quarter -
the Ajuntament (city hall) and Generalitat (regional government).

The Eixample, the city's 19thC extension or 'new town', contains one
of its most popular tourist attractions, the Temple de la Sagrada Família,
the most famous work of the great architect Antoni Gaudí (see **A-Z**).
This district has many other Modernist buildings and a large selection
of smart shops and boutiques. On the south of the city Montjuïc hill has
the Olympic stadium, other sports facilities, gardens, an amusement
park, a castle, fountains and two outstanding museums: the Museu
d'Art de Catalunya, which contains an exceptional collection of
Romanesque (see **A-Z**) and Gothic pieces (0900-1400 Tues.-Sun.); and
the Fundació Joan Miró, a cultural centre with displays of the artist's
works. Nearby is the Poble Espanyol, a mock village with copies of
buildings and *plaças* representative of Spain's architectural heritage.
Lastly, there are Las Ramblas, the city's lively tree-lined boulevards,
always bursting with vitality (see **WALK 3**).

Girona

The enchanting provincial capital is less than 40 km from resorts like Lloret de Mar, Platja d'Aro and L'Escala (see **RESORTS**, **A-Z**). It is well worth taking at least one day off from the beach to see Girona's notable sights, walk its narrow streets and browse in its shops and markets. The city is also ideal as a base for visiting all of the Costa Brava and Girona province. If you linger into the evening, or stay overnight, you will see few other tourists and be able to explore the old quarter in a haunting amber glow, or admire the town's floodlit monuments.

Girona has long been guardian of the principal route from Europe into the peninsula. The town was founded by the Iberians on the hill site above the Riu Onyar where it meets the larger Riu Ter. In the 1stC BC under the Romans it was known as Gerunda. The medieval town became an important commercial and cultural centre, and a renowned school of Cabalistic studies flourished within its Jewish quarter. Due to its strategic position, Girona has faced many onslaughts in different uprisings and wars, and is known as the 'city of a thousand sieges'. For seven months in 1809 Gironins held off the army of Napoleon.

Careful restoration has ensured that Girona contains some of the most evocative Romanesque (see **A-Z**), Gothic and Baroque architecture in Spain. Dominating the landscape is the Gothic Catedral de Girona, begun in 1312 and completed in the 16thC, one of the largest Gothic vaulted buildings in the world (see **BUILDINGS 2**, **WALK 1**, **A-Z**). The cathedral museum (see **MUSEUMS 2**) houses various notable items including a 10thC *Apocalypse*. Nearby is the church of Sant Feliu (see **BUILDINGS 2**). From the cathedral square the Passeig Arqueològic (see **HISTORIC SITES**) provides an interesting route around various sights of the Old Town including the Banys Arabs (see **BUILDINGS 2**, **WALK 1**), and the Romanesque churches of Sant Pere and Sant Nicolau (see **BUILDINGS 2**, **WALK 1**). There is less to see in the newer commercial and residential district of the Eixample, but where the Riu Onyar and Riu Ter meet is the attractive Parc de la Devesa, and the area has good boutiques, antique and shoe shops (see **MARKETS**, **SHOPPING 2**). Girona also hosts various cultural events during the summer and the Corpus Christi procession is quite an experience. A stroll on the Rambla Llibertat is a favourite pastime of visitors and locals on warm evenings. There is little nightlife but some restaurants (see **RESTAURANTS 1**) are worth a visit.

EXCURSION 4

Montserrat

1 day. *50 km north west of Barcelona following the A 2, A 11 and then the C 1411. Direct rail link from Barcelona to the mountain cableway.*

The saw-toothed massif of Montserrat, rising incongruously and almost magically above the surrounding countryside and Riu Llobregat, is one of Spain's most impressive natural sights and the spiritual heart of Catalunya (see **A-Z**).

Its growth as a religious centre, so significant for Catalans and for Catholics everywhere, began in 880 with the discovery in a cave of the small statue, *La Moreneta*, the Black Virgin. Legend claims it was carved by St Luke and first hidden by St Peter. In 976, the Benedictines were charged with its protection and they began building their monastery which by the 15thC became an independent abbey.

A multitude of miracles was attributed to this Virgin. Many rulers and notable figures made the pilgrimage to her, and St Ignatius Loyola spent some time here. Now, she receives more tourists than pilgrims. Many Catalan baby girls are still christened Montserrat and couples go to receive her blessing on their marriage. During times of suppression of their national identity, notably under Franco, the Virgin, the monks and their institution offered Catalans hope and succour. Napoleon's troops had sacked the monastery in 1811, the Carlists had suppressed it in 1835, and its end seemed final, but it survived and today some 300 monks inhabit the new, barrack-like buildings.

In the Basilica (which dates from 1560-92), *La Moreneta* (the image on display at the present dates from the 12thC) has a chamber above the high altar and the crystal voices of the boy's choir, La Escolania, ring in their daily performance of the *salve* at 1300 (except July). There is a museum with minor paintings by old masters and another exhibition area for 19thC Catalan artists.

Most rewarding for many visitors is escaping the crowds and discovering the mountain - its quiet paths, grand vistas and isolated hermitages - on foot, by funicular or cable car. It is an hour's walk to Sant Jeromi, the hermitage near the summit (1253 m), or a quick ride in the cable car. The monks run two good hostelries. There are also shops, a market, a camp site, and a youth hostel.

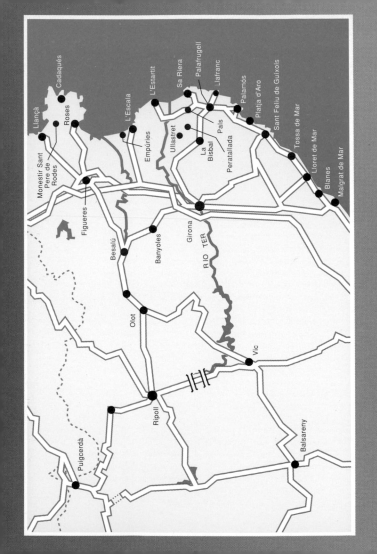

TOSSA DE MAR 39 km south east of Girona.
The Vila Vella (Old Town) on the hillside preserves its cobbled streets and quaint buildings within 12thC fortified walls. See **RESORTS 1**, **A-Z**.

PALS 39 km east of Girona.
The medieval core is pedestrianized, with narrow lanes, a Romanesque church, a round tower and medieval walls. See **TOWNS & VILLAGES 1**, **A-Z**.

PERATALLADA 9 km west of Pals.
Unspoilt, medieval walled village with privately restored castle. Nearby Vulpellac has a similar castle. See **TOWNS & VILLAGES 1**, **A-Z**.

ULLASTRET 5 km north of Peratallada.
•Museum 1030-1300, 1600-2000 Tues.-Sun.
Medieval village commanding superb views of the surrounding plain. Excavations here have revealed traces of an Iberian settlement. See **A-Z**.

EMPÚRIES 1 km north of L'Escala.
•0900-2000 Tues.-Sun. (1000-1300, 1400-1700 winter).
Excavations of a 6thC BC Greek settlement revealing temples, houses, shops, a forum, and an amphitheatre. See **EXCURSION 1**, **A-Z**.

MONESTIR SANT PERE DE RODES Serra de Roda, north of Roses.
•0900-1300, 1500-sunset. Access from Vilajuïga, also untarred road from El Port de la Selva.
Substantial 10th-11thC remains of a fortified monastery and church in a spectacular setting. Superb views from Castell de Sant Salvador. See **A-Z**.

BESALÚ 14 km north west of Banyoles.
Virtually unspoilt 11th-13thC town. Small churches, a fortified bridge and the mikwà *(Jewish ritual bath). See* **EXCURSION 1**, **TOWNS & VILLAGES 2**, **A-Z**.

GIRONA
The Passeig Arqueològic is an archeological walk visiting the historic sights of the Old Town. See **EXCURSION 3**, **TOWNS & VILLAGES 1**, **WALK 1**, **A-Z**.

Many of the resorts and inland towns have food markets, usually weekday mornings, and sometimes in the evenings.

BLANES Llotja del Peix.
•From 1630 Mon.-Fri.
Fascinating scenes as auctioneers rapidly sell off the daily catch of fish from local boats. See **RESORTS 1**, **A-Z**.

PALAMÓS Llotja del Moll.
•After 1700 Mon.-Fri.
Watch the big fleet of colourful boats come in and fishermen rush their trays of varied seafood to auctioneers who appear to conduct the sales without pausing to take breath. See **RESORTS 1**, **A-Z**.

GIRONA Mercat Municipal, Pl Calvet.
•0800-1300 Mon.-Fri.
Big, bustling and colourful market for all fresh foods. See **EXCURSION 3**, **TOWNS & VILLAGES 1**, **WALK 2**, **A-Z**.

PALAFRUGELL Pl Josep Pla.
•Third Sunday of the month (mornings).
Local antiques, crafts and fleamarket. Similar markets take place in many other towns on the Costa Brava. Ask at your local tourist office for details. See **TOWNS & VILLAGES 1**, **A-Z**.

GIRONA Passeig de la Devesa.
•Tuesday and Saturday mornings.
Biggest of the weekly markets for household goods, clothes, some crafts and junk. Watch your pockets and purse. See **EXCURSION 3**, **TOWNS & VILLAGES 1**, **A-Z**.

FIGUERES Passeig Nou.
•Thursday mornings.
Mainly agricultural produce. Involves animated sales of livestock and tools. See **EXCURSION 1**, **A-Z**.

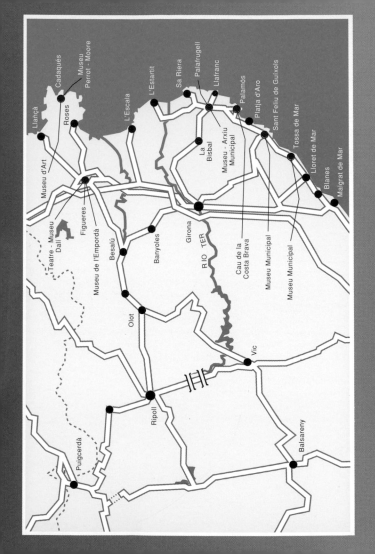

MUSEU MUNICIPAL Vila Vella, Tossa de Mar.
•1000-1300, 1630-1900.
In a medieval house, a small, mixed collection ranges from Roman artefacts to recent works of local artists. Also works by Chagall, Klein, Metzinger.

MUSEU MUNICIPAL Pl de Monestir, Sant Feliu de Guíxols.
•1100-1300, 1700-2000.
*In an annexe of the monastery (see **BUILDINGS 1**) is a small collection of Roman, Greek and Iberian exhibits unearthed locally.*

CAU DE LA COSTA BRAVA Pl del Forn, Palamós.
•1000-1300, 1600-1830.
Fascinating jumble of curiosities including items relating to the cork industry, a large snail collection, coins and sailors' gear.

MUSEU-ARXIU MUNICIPAL Av Josep Pla, Palafrugell.
•1700-2000.
*Exhibits tracing the history of the local industry based on cork (see **A-Z**).*

MUSEU D'ART Monturiol, Cadaqués.
•1200-1400, 1700-1900. Closed Sun. pm.
Contemporary works in a range of styles by local artists.

MUSEU PERROT-MOORE Pl Frederic Rahola, Cadaqués.
•1700-2100; 1100-1300 (Aug.).
Small collection of 15th to 20thC European paintings.

TEATRE-MUSEU DALÍ Pl Gala Salvador Dalí, Figueres.
•0900-2015 (summer), 1130-1715 (winter).
Surrealist experience created by the town's most famous son. Madman's nonsense or meaningful art? Well worth a visit to decide for yourself. See **EXCURSION 1**, **Dalí**.

MUSEU DE L'EMPORDÀ Rambla 1, Figueres.
•1100-1300, 1630-2000 Tues.-Sun.
Local archeology, art and historical exhibits. See **EXCURSION 1**.

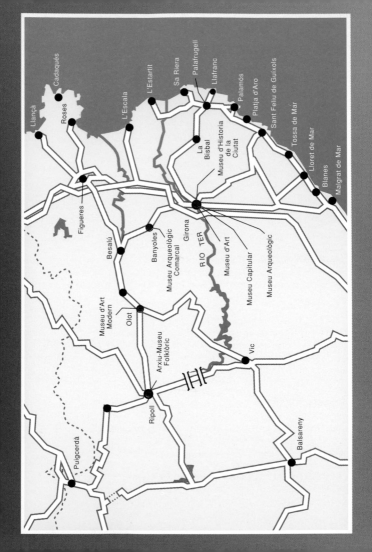

MUSEU D'ART MODERN Torre Castanys (El Parc), Olot.
• 1100-1300, 1600-1800.
Paintings of 19th and 20thC Catalan artists and works of the Olot School.

ARXIU-MUSEU FOLKLÒRIC Monestir de Santa María, Ripoll.
• 0900-1300, 1500-1900.
History and culture of the Ripoll comarca (district). See 16th-17thC firearms for which the region gained a great reputation throughout Europe.

MUSEU ARQUEOLÒGIC COMARCAL Pl de la Font, Banyoles.
• 1000-1300, 1600-1900 Tues.-Sun.
This notable building houses local archeological finds.

MUSEU D'HISTORIA DE LA CIUTAT Força, Ciutat Vella, Girona.
1000-1400, 1700-1900 Tues.-Sun. (Closed Sun. & hol. pm).
In the Antic Convent de Sant Antoni are prehistoric objects, items relating to the city's industrial history, instruments and materials relating to the sardana (see A-Z). See WALK 1.

MUSEU D'ART Palau Episcopal, Pl Lledoners, Ciutat Vella, Girona.
1000-1300, 1630-1900 Tues.-Sun. (Closed Sun. and hol. pm).
Well-displayed Romanesque (see A-Z) and Gothic exhibits show the development of Catalan art in the medieval period. See WALK 1.

MUSEU CAPITULAR Catedral, Ciutat Vella, Girona.
1000-1300, 1630-1900 Tues.-Sat.
*The Beatus de Girona, an illuminated document from AD 975, and the Tapís de la Creació, a rare 12thC tapestry, are the outstanding exhibits among a rich collection of religious items. See **Catedral de Girona**.*

MUSEU ARQUEOLÒGIC Església Sant Pere de Galligants, Girona.
1000-1300, 1630-1900 Tues.-Sun. (Closed Sun. and hol. pm).
Archeological finds from Girona province are displayed in the church and cloister of this Romanesque ensemble which backs onto part of the old city walls. Worth visiting for the building as well as the exhibits. See WALK 1.

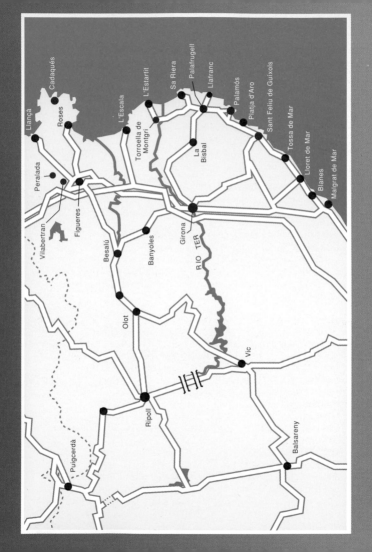

SANT FELIU DE GUÍXOLS Halfway between Tossa de Mar and Palamós.
•July-Aug.
Festival Internacional de Música de la Porta Ferrada. A small programme of performances in the parish church. See **A-Z**.

PALAMÓS Halfway between Palafrugell and Sant Feliu de Guíxols.
•July-Sept.
Another similar Festival Internacional de Música. See **A-Z**.

TORROELLA DE MONTGRI 5 km inland from L'Estartit.
•June-Aug.
Festival Internacional de Música. Ten events feature lesser-known international soloists and chamber orchestras. Musical interpretation courses for young people from mid-July to the end of August.

CADAQUÉS
•July-Aug.
Festival Internacional de Música de Cadaqués. Varied programme of classics with top performers, young musicians and contemporary works. See **A-Z**.

PERALADA 6 km north east of Figueres.
•Mid-July to mid-Aug.
Based at the Casino Peralada (see **NIGHTLIFE**), *this programme of music and dance features top performers like Montserrat Caballé. See* **A-Z**.

VILABERTRAN 2 km north of Figueres.
•June-July.
Festival Internacional de Música de l'Empordà. Mostly local performers present five concerts in the church. Other cultural events in the old monastery.

GIRONA
Lively cultural scene all year for Catalan speakers, but music, dance and some theatre present no language problems. See what's on at Centre Cultural la Mercè, Casa de Cultura Lorenzana, Fontana d'Or, Teatre Municipal and Església de Sant Feliu. See **Music**, **A-Z**.

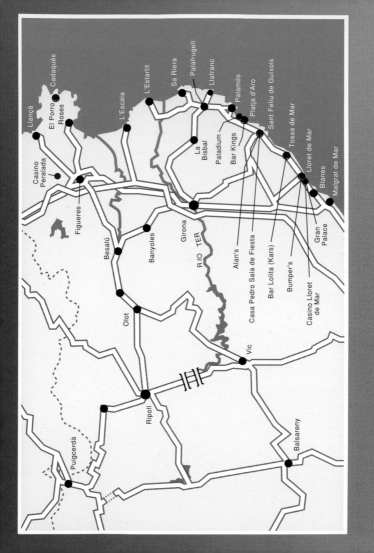

The largest and most lively choice of nightlife is in Lloret de Mar and Platja d'Aro, and you'll soon discover a favourite bar or disco. Here is a selection.

BUMPER'S Sant Lluc 2, Lloret de Mar.
Grill bar, four tropical bars, two glass dance floors and a boutique.

GRAN PALACE Ctra Blanes km 1.4, Lloret de Mar.
*Venue for international cabaret and commercial flamenco (see **A-Z**) shows.*

CASINO LLORET DE MAR Crta Blanes, Lloret de Mar.
Dining and gambling. Passport essential for entry to gaming rooms.

BAR LOLITA (KARS) Sant Elm 17, Tossa de Mar.
Popular bar with a South American ambience.

ALAN'S Sant Llorenç 16, Sant Feliu de Guíxols.
Genial bar which also serves tasty food.

CASA PEDRO SALA DE FIESTA Trav Call 6, Sant Feliu de Guíxols.
*Unpretentious place which presents good flamenco (see **A-Z**) shows.*

BAR KINGS Ctra San Feliu, Platja D'Aro.
Big screen video bar and summer terrassa *where bronzed beauties gather at the start of the night.*

PALADIUM Ctra Palamós, Platja D'Aro.
Disco dancing, food and drink until the sun rises in one of the Costa Brava's top summer nightspots.

EL PORRO Portal de la Font 1, Cadaqués.
Lively disco bar with an arty, uninhibited crowd.

CASINO PERALADA Castell de Peralada.
Converted 15thC castle with bar, restaurant and gambling (passport required). See **MUSIC & DANCE**.

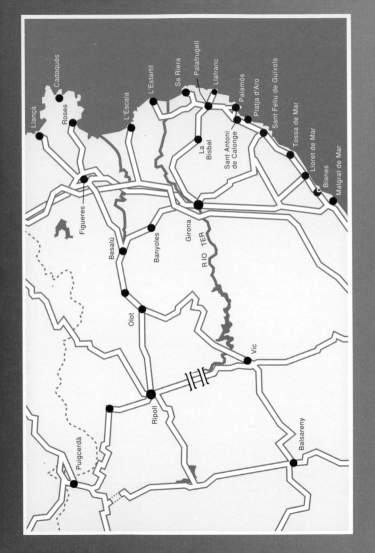

BLANES

5 km south of Lloret de Mar.
Attractive, spacious resort with a wide choice of accommodation and good beaches. Local sights include the botanic gardens. See **MARKETS**, **A-Z**.

LLORET DE MAR

44 km south of Girona.
A once small fishing village now given over to high-rise apartments and mass tourism. Pulsating nightlife (see **NIGHTLIFE***) and sandy beach. See* **A-Z**.

TOSSA DE MAR

13 km north of Lloret de Mar. 35 km south east of Girona.
Dramatic fortified old town (see **HISTORIC SITES***), attractive new town centre, good restaurants and shops, clear waters, sheltered beaches. See* **A-Z**.

SANT FELIU DE GUÍXOLS

35 km south east of Girona.
A touch of class pervades this town and resort, enhanced by the exclusive S'Agaró residential area (see **BUILDINGS 1***). Shaded esplanade and Ramblas with elegant buildings. Good restaurants (see* **RESTAURANTS 2***). See* **A-Z**.

PLATJA D'ARO

Halfway between Palamós and Sant Feliu de Guíxols.
A purpose-built resort which vies with Lloret as the coast's liveliest. Rows of apartment blocks face directly onto an extensive beach. The main road is packed with shops, restaurants (see **RESTAURANTS 2***) and cafés. See* **A-Z**.

SANT ANTONI DE CALONGE

4 km south of Palamós.
A mix of smaller hotels, apartments, villas, camp sites and shops continues the ribbon development along this part of the coast.

PALAMÓS

49 km south east of Girona.
Hardworking fishing and commercial port with growing tourism based on small hotels and private apartments. See **MARKETS**, **A-Z**.

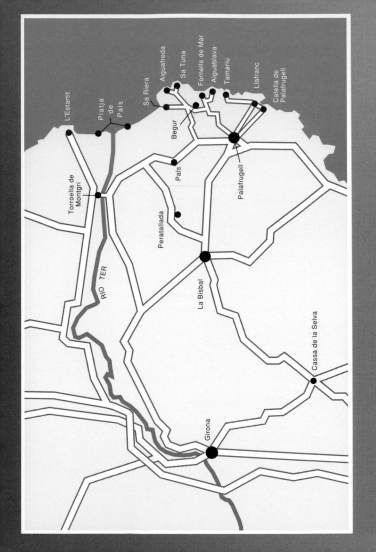

CALELLA DE PALAFRUGELL

5 km south of Palafrugell.
The first of a batch of small, quiet resorts along this part of the coast up to Sa Riera. Choice of five delightful, small beaches. See **Palafrugell**.

LLAFRANC

5 km south of Palafrugell.
Less pretty than its neighbours, but a wide sweep of beach. See **Palafrugell**.

TAMARIU

5 km south of Palafrugell.
Smallest of Palafrugell's three resorts, it has retained much of its charm. To the north is Aigua-Xellida, barely touched by development. See **Palafrugell**.

AIGUABLAVA / FORNELLS DE MAR

Begur.
Two beach resorts of Begur (see **TOWNS AND VILLAGES 1**, **A-Z***). Luxury villas hide in the pines above these idyllic coves with small sandy beaches.*

SA TUNA / AIGUAFREDA

Near Begur.
Unspoilt coves with accommodation. See **TOWNS & VILLAGES 1**, **Begur**.

SA RIERA

5 km east of Pals.
Fishing hamlet and unpretentious small resort for quiet holidays.

PLATJA DE PALS

North of Sa Riera.
Large scale development of villas, apartments and services. Long, wide beach stretches northwards. Ugly radio masts mar the views. See **Pals**.

L'ESTARTIT

Just north of the Riu Ter estuary.
Family resort of big apartment blocks, medium and small hotels. The long beach has all facilities, and there is also a pleasure port. See **A-Z**.

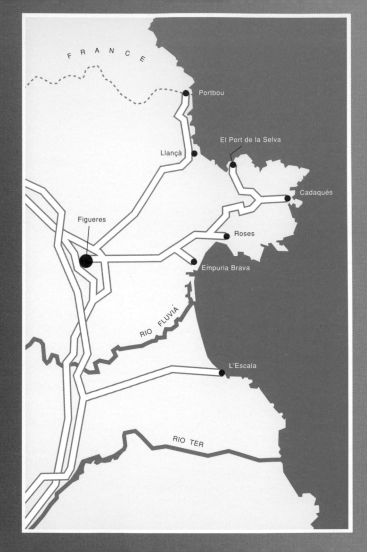

L'ESCALA

56 km north east of Girona.
Fishing village with the smaller hotels in centre and villas and apartment blocks spreading south to lovely Cala Montgó. Good choice of beaches and water sports. See **A-Z**.

EMPURIA BRAVA

South of Roses.
Integrated, low-rise holiday village based on a system of canals. One hotel, many private villas. Long beach, good sports facilities.

ROSES

Northern end of the Golf de Roses.
Grand setting at head of the bay. Once a Greek colony, now a fishing port and international resort. The waterfront is attractive and there are fine beaches to east of the town. See **A-Z**.

CADAQUÉS

On the Cap de Creus peninsula, 36 km east of Figueres.
A picturesque tumble of whitewashed buildings fringe a small bay at the end of the bleak Cap de Creus. See **A-Z**.

EL PORT DE LA SELVA

13 km north of Cadaqués.
A fishing village situated on a horseshoe bay which has an open beach and limited tourist development.

LLANÇÀ

14 km south of the French border.
Inland vila twinned with its port. Fishing and sports harbour. The surrounding coast offers a choice of beaches, pebbly or coarse sand.

PORTBOU

On the French border.
Railway yards dominate this unassuming working town with modest tourist amenities. It features a pleasant grey sand/pebble beach.

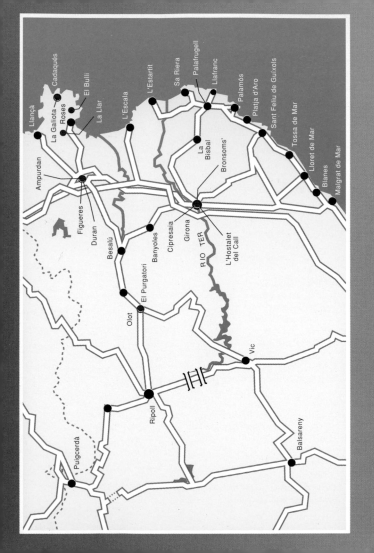

North

LA LLAR Ctra Roses/Figueres, Roses.
•Closed Thurs. (not July/Aug.) and 2nd fortnight in Nov. •Moderate.
Pleasant atmosphere, good-quality food and fair prices.

EL BULLI Cala Montjoi, Roses.
•Closed Mon./Tues. lunch (not July/Aug.), 15 Jan.-15 Mar. •Expensive.
Elegant decor, swish service and superb food.

LA GALIOTA Narcis Monturiol 9, Cadaqués.
•Open daily (June-Oct.), weekends only (Nov.-May). •Inexpensive.
Pepita serves, sister Nuri cooks with flair. Seafood is a speciality.

AMPURDAN Ctra N II, km 1.5 (road to motorway), Figueres.
•Moderate.
This hotel restaurant deserves its enviable reputation for careful, classical cooking of regional dishes. The menu of the day offers good value.

DURAN Lasauca 5, Figueres.
•Moderate.
Hotel restaurant serving top quality regional dishes.

EL PURGATORI Bisbe Serra 58, Olot.
•Closed Sun. night, Mon. and 2nd fortnight in July. •Moderate.
Small choice of creative dishes with local and Basque inspiration.

CIPRESAIA Carreras Peralta 5, Girona.
•Closed Sun. •Moderate.
The city's long-standing top spot for serious eating.

L'HOSTALET DEL CALL Travesia Oliva i Prat 4, Girona.
•Closed Mon. (not Apr.-Sept.) and Nov. •Moderate.
Traditional cooking in the heart of the medieval Jewish quarter.

BRONSOMS' Av Sant Francesc 7, Girona.
•Closed Sat., Sun. nights and 1st fortnight in Aug. •Inexpensive.
Simple cooking in large portions. A speciality is suquet de peix.

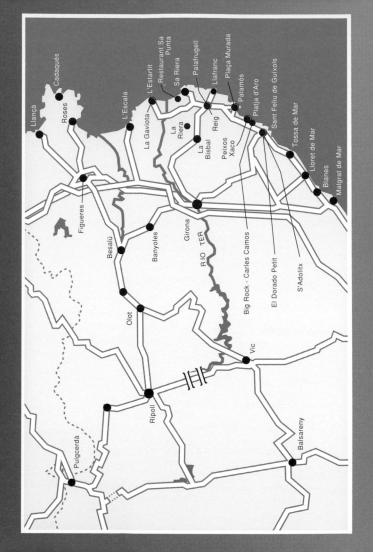

Central

EL DORADO PETIT Rambla Vidal 11, Sant Feliu de Guixols.
•Closed Wed. (Oct.-Apr.) and Nov. • Expensive-Moderate.
Traditional recipes, lightened by new wave Mediterranean cooking.

S'ADOLITX Mayor 13, Sant Feliu de Guíxols.
•Closed Nov.-Feb. •Moderate-Inexpensive.
No-nonsense cooking, decor and service. Quiet, covered terrace.

BIG ROCK - CARLES CAMOS Barri de Fanals 5, Platja D'Aro.
•Closed Mon. •Moderate-Expensive.
Excellent classic and modern seafood (and meat) dishes.

PEIXOS XACO Ctra Sant Feliu (corner c/ Rocosa), Platja D'Aro.
•Closed Sun. •Inexpensive.
Fresh seafood simply prepared for eating indoors or outside.

PLAÇA MURADA Pl Murada 5, Palamós.
•Closed Mon. (15 Oct.-16 June) and Nov. •Inexpensive.
Good choice among the many seafood eateries in Palamós. It's pretty, with views of the port and bay. Friendly, efficient service. Summer terrace.

REIG Torres Jonama 53, Palafrugell.
•Closed Sun. night and Mon. in winter. •Inexpensive.
Straightforward, hearty helpings of local fare. A firm favourite with locals.

RESTAURANT SA PUNTA Urb Sa Punta, Platja de Pals.
•Closed Mon and 15 Jan.-15 Feb. •Moderate.
Large, smart restaurant serving unpretentious, imaginative cuisine.

LA RIERA Pl les Voltes, Peratallada.
•Closed Mon. (winter) and Dec.-Mar. •Inexpensive.
Local cuisine with a light touch. Friendly family feel. Charming and popular.

LA GAVIOTA Passeig Maritim, L'Estartit.
•Inexpensive-Moderate.
The day's menu is a good bet. Popular with families, tourists and locals.

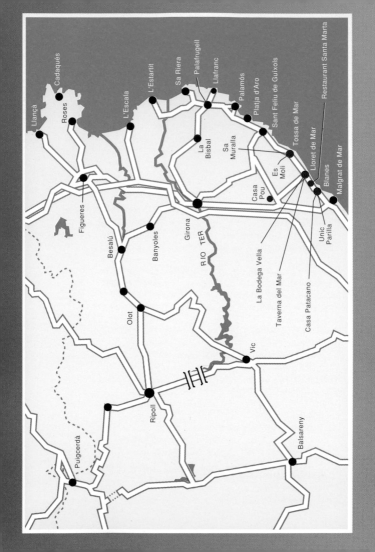

South

CASA PATACANO Passeig del Mar 12, Blanes.
•Closed Mon. (winter) and Nov. to mid-Jan. •Moderate.
Unpretentious and friendly. Justifies its high reputation for good fish dishes like planxada de peix *and* sarsuela de peix *(see* **Food***).*

UNIC PARILLA Puerta Nueva 7, Blanes.
•Closed Mon. and Dec.-6 Jan. •Moderate.
Simple decor and unfussy preparation of what's best from the market.

LA BODEGA VELLA Na Marina 14, Lloret de Mar.
•Closed Nov. to Feb. •Expensive.
The international menu has a few regional specialities.

RESTAURANT SANTA MARTA Platja Santa Cristina, Lloret de Mar.
•Closed 15 Dec.-20 Jan. •Expensive.
International, Spanish and regional dishes with a special menu for children.

TAVERNA DEL MAR Pescadors 5, Lloret de Mar.
•Closed Nov.-Mar. •Inexpensive.
A rustic tavern with hints of old Lloret and which offers plain cooking of staple Catalan dishes, mainly fish.

SA MURALLA Portal 16, Tossa de Mar.
•Inexpensive-Moderate.
A well-sited, pretty and lively place. Enjoy the friendly service and the many good plats catalans, *including the freshest of seafood.*

ES MOLI Tarull 3, Tossa de Mar.
•Closed Mon. and Nov.-Mar. •Moderate.
Scores higher for the romantic setting around the patio garden than for its menu. Try it on a relaxed summer's evening.

CASA POU Pau Casals 15, Vidreres.
•Closed Mon. (winter). •Moderate.
Country restaurant serving fresh food prepared the traditional way.

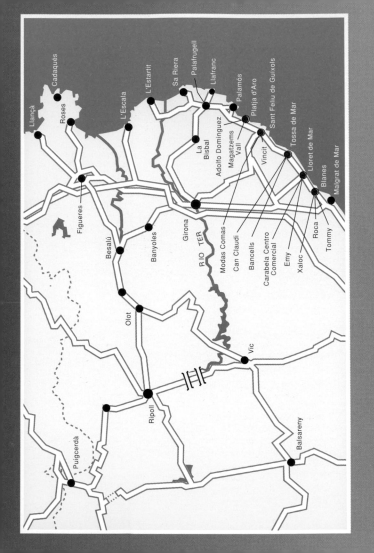

ROCA Ample 4, Blanes.
Wide stocks of Lladró and other high-quality ceramics.

XALOC Mercaders 12, Blanes.
A good selection of smart footwear and leather accessories.

TOMMY Passeig de Dintre 12, Blanes.
Small unisex boutique with trendy, quality fashions.

CARABELA CENTRO COMERCIAL Ferrán Agulló, Lloret de Mar.
Three floors of up-market shops including many boutiques.

EMY Venecia 1, Lloret de Mar.
Selection of good-quality leather and fur fashions.

BANCELLS Pou de la Vila 1, Tossa de Mar.
Fine craftsmanship in iron, ceramics and glass.

CAN CLAUDI Av Costa Brava 28, Tossa de Mar.
Wine from the barrel, spirits and liqueurs. No. 20 has cheeses, etc.

MODAS COMAS de la Rutlla 8, Sant Feliu de Guíxols.
Own manufacture and good stocks of jackets, coats, gloves, handbags, in leather and suede.

VINCIT Mossèn Cinto Verdaguer 17, Sant Feliu de Guíxols.
*Antiques, lovely dried flowers, wickerwork, and quality Dalí (see **A-Z**) reproductions on different materials.*

ADOLFO DOMINGUEZ El Carillon, Ctra de San Feliu, Platja D'Aro.
Fashion by one of Spain's top designers in a small mall which includes other worthwhile shops. Another is Galerías San Luis on the same road.

MAGATZEMS VALL Ctra de Sant Feliu 8, Platja D'Aro.
Neat mini-department store.

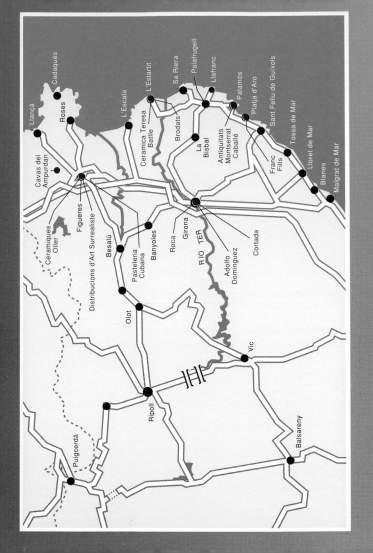

FRANC FILLS Ctra de San Feliu 22, Platja D'Aro.
Big choice of leatherwear and furs. Daily fashion shows in summer. There are other similar shops along this street.

ANTIQUITATS MONTSERRAT CABALLÉ Major 21, Palamós.
Porcelain, wood sculptures, Manises ceramics, fans, bronze work, paintings.

CERAMICA TERESA BATLLE Església 36, L'Estartit.
Ceramic plates, vases, jugs and fruit bowls made in its own workshop.

BRODATS Santa Anna 43, L'Estartit.
Mostly hand-embroidered tablecloths, handkerchiefs, shawls and fans.

CAVAS DEL AMPURDAN Peralada.
The region's wines supplied by local bodegas.

DISTRIBUCIONS D'ART SURREALISTE Pl Gala i Dalí, Figueres.
*Posters, prints and postcards of Dalí's works (see **A-Z**).*

CERAMIQUES OLLER Sant Pere 3, Figueres.
Artesania which sells popular Catalan ceramics from its own workshop.

PASTELERIA CUBANA Nou 5, Figueres.
Good place for cream-filled xuxos and other tempting pastries.

ROCA Mercaders 2 and Migdia 7, Girona.
Fresh chocolates, toffees and bonbons, prettily gift-packed.

ADOLFO DOMINGUEZ Santa Clara 60, Girona.
Top designer-label clothes and accessories for both sexes in a street full of fashion shops.

CORTADA Nou 11, Girona.
Barcelona-style women's fashion boutique. Also has branches in Figueres, Banyoles and Platja d'Aro.

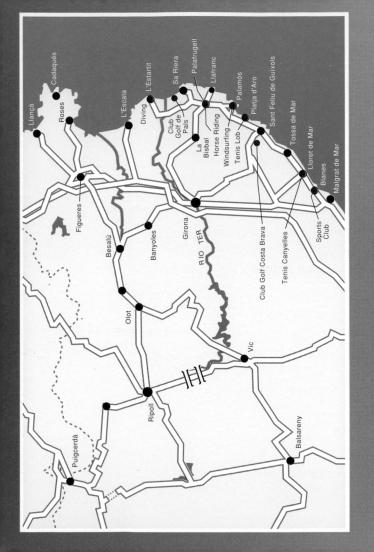

SPORTS CLUB
Pavelló Esportiu Municipal, Passeig S'Abanell, Blanes.
Basketball, indoor football, handball, volleyball, roller hockey, judo, gym.
Facilities are available to foreign teams for off-season practice. Other larger
resorts have similar amenities.

TENNIS
Tenis Canyelles, Cala Canyelles, Lloret de Mar.
This multi-sports centre includes tennis, pelota, gym, swimming pool,
bar/restaurant and games room. Organizes horse riding and climbing trips.

Tenis Lob, Víctor Català, Platja D'Aro.
Four cement courts. Lessons and tournaments for all levels. Trampolines.
Also, Club Tenis D'Aro, 12 clay courts.

WINDSURFING
Escola de Vela Solomar, Platja de Palamós, Palamós.
Sailing and windsurfing school which provides tuition for all ages.

HORSE RIDING
Club Hipic Baix Empordà, Barri de Santa Margarita, Palafrugell.
Horse riding opportunities. Also Hipica La Fanga, Ctra de Girona. See **A-Z**.

DIVING L'Estartit.
Several operators provide all the gear, and boats, for exploring the under-
water beauty around the Illes Medes. There are organized diving groups.

GOLF
Club Golf Costa Brava, La Masia, 17246 Santa Cristina D'Aro.
18 holes. Bar, restaurant, shop, hire facilities.
The first nine holes are hilly among oaks and pines with narrow fairways;
the inward nine is flatter, with wider fairways.

Club Golf de Pals, Platja de Pals, 17256 Pals.
18 holes. Bar, restaurant, shop, hire facilities.
A flat course in a pine wood close to beach. Tough if the tramontana *blows.*

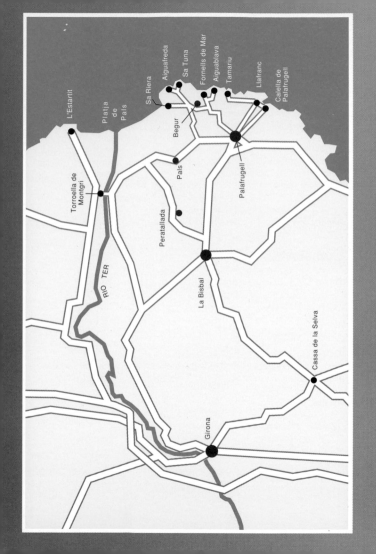

GIRONA
Enchanting provincial capital of 87,000 inhabitants. It's a 'must' destination at the nub of the Costa Brava's communications network with outstanding sights and good shopping. See **EXCURSION 3, WALKS 1 & 2, A-Z**.

LA BISBAL 27 km east of Girona.
Capital of the Baix Empordà region, with a population of 8000. Makes its living from commerce, agriculture and its ceramics industry. See **CRAFTS & CUSTOMS, A-Z**.

PALAFRUGELL 42 km east of Girona.
Includes the resorts of Calella, Tamariu and Llafranc within its municipal boundary (see **RESORTS 2**). *The resident population is 15,000. Now a busy agricultural, commercial and light industrial centre, it grew rich at the height of the prosperity of the cork industry (see* **A-Z**) *and has a number of Modernist buildings. Good food shops and restaurants. See* **A-Z**.

BEGUR 6 km north of Palafrugell.
Hilltop castle ruins add drama to this chic little town of many porticoed buildings, much whitewash and reddish tiles. It serves the small resorts of Aiguablava, Fornells, Sa Tuna, Aiguafreda and Sa Riera (see **RESORTS 2**). *The area has quite a large, and growing, expatriate population. See* **A-Z**.

PALS 9 km north west of Begur.
A private initiative was begun in 1948 to restore its ruined medieval buildings and fortifications. Thirty years later and with official funding the work was completed. It has been beautifully done and is best seen in the early morning or in the evening. The newer town sprawls below and 5 km away is Platja de Pals (see **RESORTS 2**), *its growing resort area. See* **HISTORIC SITES, A-Z**.

PERATALLADA 9 km west of Pals.
Some of this fortified village's Gothic structures have been finely restored, others not, and still serve farming uses. An ageless, sleepy place to stroll. Its restaurants are popular with Gironins. See **HISTORIC SITES, A-Z**.

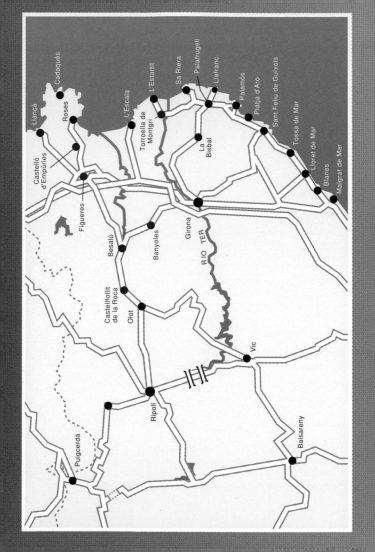

FIGUERES 35 km north of Girona.
Capital and market town of the Alt Empordà comarca. Its 30,000 inhabitants get swamped by visitors to Dalí's museum (see MUSEUMS 1*). Besides that, there is a pleasant Rambla, a pedestrian area, a fair range of shops (see* SHOPPING 2*), good restaurants, worthwhile museums (see* CHILDREN, MUSEUMS 1*), art exhibitions and noteworthy buildings (see* BUILDINGS 1*). See* EXCURSION 1, A-Z.

TORROELLA DE MONTGRI 6 km from the mouth of the Riu Ter.
Its ruined castle on a peak of the Montgri massif is a landmark which can be seen from afar. Riu Ter flows slowly through agricultural land past the busy small town. Linger here a while and be delighted by its colourful daily life. The town's port and resort is L'Estartit (see RESORTS 2, A-Z*), 5 km away.*

CASTELLÓ D'EMPÚRIES 8 km east of Figueres.
Impressive monumental quarter of noble buildings, gate and towers which has the mini-cathedral of Santa Maria (see BUILDINGS 1*) as centrepiece. A notable bridge spans the Riu Muga. Empuria Brava (see* RESORTS 3*) is in its municipality.*

BANYOLES 20 km north west of Girona.
There is some light industry here but the town's 12,000 people are mostly involved in servicing the agricultural sector and summertime visitors who flock to its lake (see CHILDREN*). Don't miss the arcaded square, monastery and small museums (see* MUSEUMS 2*) or the exceptional Romanesque (see* A-Z*) church of Santa Maria at nearby Porqueres. See* EXCURSION 1.

BESALÚ 14 km north west of Banyoles.
Once you've seen it, you'll never forget this ancient town. It bravely resists onslaughts of tourists to retain its haunting character. See EXCURSION 1, A-Z.

CASTELLFOLLIT DE LA ROCA 16 km west of Besalú.
Atop a 60 m high basalt spur into the Riu Fluvià, this fairy-tale walled town of narrow streets and ancient houses is another of the region's unforgettable sights. Best viewed from the Besalú side of the C 150 road. The steep cliff-side is often floodlit to great effect.

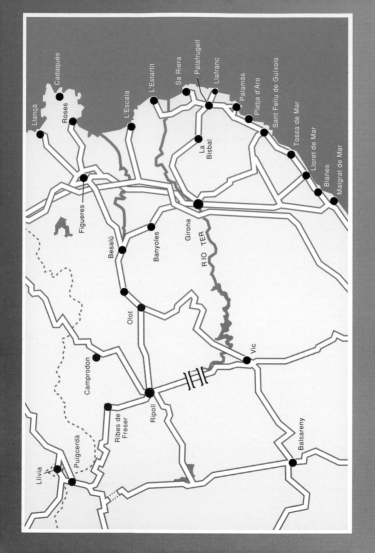

OLOT 60 km north west of Girona.
Population 25,000. The capital of Garrotxa and a town which thrives on the district's agriculture, livestock rearing and industry (mainly textile). Don't be put off by the ugly outskirts - the streets have a pleasant atmosphere and there are buildings, crafts shops and museums to visit. See **BUILDINGS 2, CRAFTS & CUSTOMS, MUSEUMS 2.**

CAMPRODON 24 km north east of Ripoll.
The 'Emerald of the Pyrenees' lies amidst a patchwork of woods and meadows where the sound of water is ever present. It is a beautiful and typical mountain village with a 16thC hump-backed bridge across the brisk Riu Ter, a maze of narrow lanes, Romanesque (see **A-Z***) churches and other handsome buildings. Nearby are the restored 11thC Monestir Sant Pere, other pretty villages and ski slopes.*

RIPOLL 86 km west of Girona.
Population 12,000. There's some light industry in the capital of the mainly agricultural El Ripolles district. Its historic and impressive monastery draws the crowds. See **BUILDINGS 2, MUSEUMS 2, Santa Maria de Ripoll**.

RIBES DE FRESER
This welcoming village serves as a staging post for mountain-lovers during all seasons. A rack railway runs through spectacular scenery to Núria.

PUIGCERDÀ 67 km north west of Ripoll.
The capital of the mountainous La Cerdanya district is home to 6000 people. It is a popular summer resort with a leisure lake, golf course, private villas and about 20 small hotels. There is beautiful countryside to explore. Hikers, climbers and fishing enthusiasts throng here in warmer months, skiers in winter.

LLÍVIA 3 km north east of Puigcerdà.
Once the capital of La Cerdanya, this is a tiny bit of Spain surrounded by French territory following the 1659 treaty between the two nations. The population of about 1000 is swelled by holiday chalet owners in both summer and winter. View exhibits from 'Europe's oldest pharmacy'.

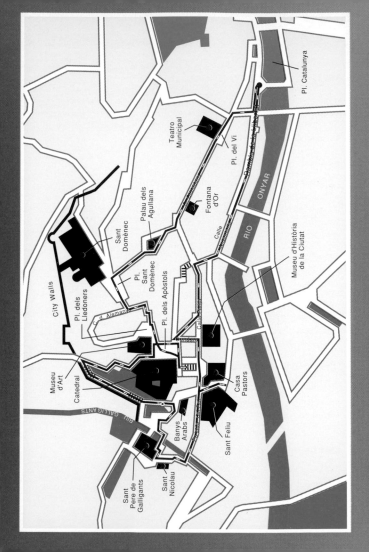

Pl. Catalunya

Teatro Municipal

Pl. del Vi

Rambla de la Llibertat

ONYAR

RIO

Palau dels Aguilana

Fontana d'Or

Sant Domènec

Calle

RIO

Museu d'Història de la Ciutat

City Walls

Pl. dels Lledoners

Pl. Sant Domènec

C. d. Alemanys

Pl. dels Apòstols

Calle Forca

Museu d'Art

Catedral

Casa Pastors

RIU GALLIGANTS

Banys Arabs

Sant Feliu

Sant Pere de Galligants

Sant Nicolau

Girona Old Town

1 hr 40 min

Start from Plaça Catalunya. Leave by the north-east corner (keeping the river to your left) and enter Rambla de la Llibertat, an attractive, shaded walkway lined on the right-hand side with medieval arcades (*voltes*) containing shops, restaurants and open-air cafés. Continue into c/ Argenteria, once famous for its metal crafts. Turn right at the end of the street and then left into c/ Força, a narrow, rising street with entrances to pretty patios, shops and eating places. This is the heart of haunting El Call, the medieval Jewish quarter. You can see more of the area by making a detour right into the tiny, steep c/ Sant Llorenç and the Escales de la Pera. Turn left into the c/ Cundaro to return to the c/ Força. Ahead is the Museu d'Història de la Ciutat (see **MUSEUMS 2**). The c/ Força ends in the splendid Plaça de la Catedral. 30 min
On the left opposite the square is the restored Casa Pastors (now Law Courts). To the right of the magnificent Baroque staircase is the striking Gothic facade of the Pia Almoina (now the College of Architects). At the top looms the Baroque facade and tower of the magnificent cathedral. Continue through the Portal de Sobreportes and turn left to enter the church of Sant Feliu by the side door (see **BUILDINGS 2**). Exit left and then turn left along the narrow Pujada del Rei, across the small R/ Galligants and then turn right. On the left is the beautiful little church of Sant Nicolau (see **BUILDINGS 2**), ahead the larger church of Sant Pere de Galligants (see **MUSEUMS 2**), both outstanding examples of Catalan Romanesque (see **A-Z**). 20 min
Exit left, and from here there is a good view of the old walls and Cornèlia and Júlia towers. Cross R/ Galligants to the Banys Arabs (see **BUILDINGS 2**). Exit and take the steps on the left to follow Passeig Arqueològic (see **HISTORIC SITES**) with its pretty views of the Vall de Sant Daniel and the walls running up to Montjuïc hill. Go through the Portal Sant Cristòfol, and down alongside the cathedral's apse to reach the Plaça dels Apòstols surrounded by imposing buildings. Visit the Museu d'Art (see **MUSEUMS 2**) in the Palau Episcopal on the left. Note the restored Gothic side doorway of the cathedral before going around to enter the cathedral by the main door (see **BUILDINGS 2**, **Catedral de Girona**). 30 min

From the cathedral cross Plaça dels Apòstols into Plaça dels Lledoners (note the 15thC fountain) and into the c/ Bellmirall. Then turn left into the c/ dels Alemanys and right into Plaça Sant Domènec, dominated by its Dominican church and convent (now part of the university). Note the Renaissance facade of Les Aiguiles. Turn right down the steps to the unforgettable urban ensemble of the church of Sant Martí Sacosta, stairways and Palau dels Agullana. Turn left into the c/ Ciutadans, with its arcades (*voltes*) of Fontana d'Or on the right. Reach Plaça del Vi with more *voltes*, the town hall, patio, and Teatre Municipal. Return to Plaça Catalunya. 20 min

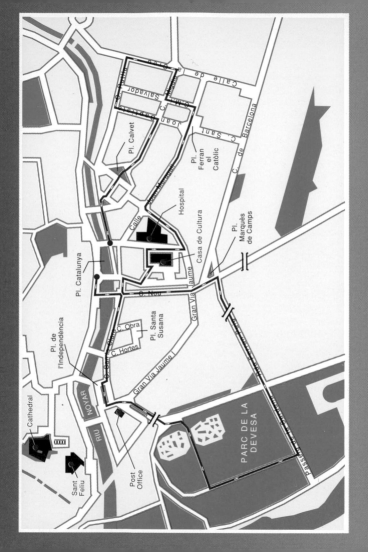

Girona New Town

1 hr 40 min
This walk is best done in the mornings, preferably on a Tuesday or Saturday.
See **MARKETS, SHOPPING**.

Start from Plaça Catalunya. Leave by the north-east corner, then turn left onto Pont de Pedra to cross the Riu Onyar. From here there is a good view of the much photographed riverside buildings and the towers of Sant Feliu and the cathedral behind. Turn right into c/ Santa Clara, a pleasant shopping area with boutiques and art galleries. You may want to make a detour left to visit the shops along the c/ Obra, Plaça Santa Susana and c/ Hortes. Santa Clara ends in Plaça de l'Independència, a lively Neoclassical style square with bars, cafés and restaurants under the arcades. Note the group statue commemorating Girona's resistance to Napoleon's seven-month siege in 1809. 20 min
Head north west into Av Ramon Folch, with the main Post Office on your right. Walk under the railway into Parc de la Devesa close to its formal gardens and walk through the lines of unusually tall plane trees towards Passeig de la Sardana. Have a stroll around the market if it's on. Go into Rda Ferran Puig. Turn left at Plaça Marquès de Camps, across Gran Via Jaume I and ahead into the lane of c/ Nou. This area boasts many tempting shops. Towards the end on the right at No 5 is the Valvi Granja Bar, ideal for a spot of refreshment. 30 min
From c/ Nou, turn right, then right again, then turn left to cross into c/ Fontanilles and reach Plaça Hospital. Immediately on your right is the Casa de Cultura (an old orphanage) with its elaborate portal set in a plain facade. Note the Constitution memorial, and ahead the old Hospital, which has an attractive courtyard. 10 min
Turn left into Gran Via Jaume I, filled with shops and offices, and then right along c/ Joan Maragall. Beyond Plaça Ferran el Catòlic is the developing shopping district of Migdia. Turn left into c/ Maluquer i Salvador, then right into c/ Migdia, left c/ de la Creu, left c/ Rutlla, and then left again into c/ Sant Joan Baptista. Turn right into c/ Migdia (from Sant Joan Baptista) and continue to Pl Calvet, the site of the municipal market with its decorative and varied displays of fresh foods (see **MARKETS**). From here it's a short walk to Plaça Catalunya, where this walk ends. 30 min

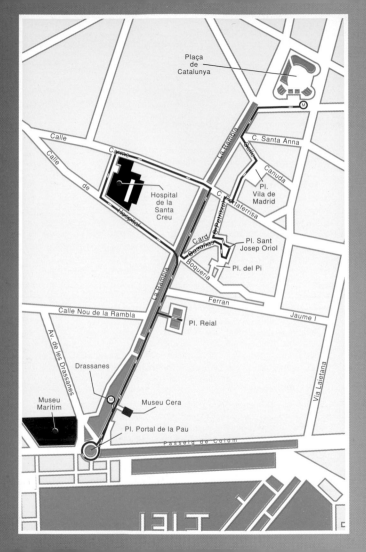

Barcelona - La Rambla

2 hr
La Rambla, a series of tree-lined boulevards, links the port with the Plaça de Catalunya. This walk makes detours from La Rambla to include more points of interest.

Start from M Plaça de Catalunya. To the right of the metro exit is the little Font de Canaletes; drink from it and, so the legend goes, you're sure to return to Barcelona. This area is a popular spot for street performers. To the left, c/ Santa Anna has good choice of snack bars. Take c/ Canuda, past the Ateneo and turn right through the quiet Pl Vila de Madrid to c/ Portaferrisa, an interesting shopping street. Follow the c/ Petritxol, which leads to Pl Sant Josep Oriol and Pl del Pi where artists and students gather in the shadow of the Gothic church. C/ Cardenal Casañas leads you back to La Rambla. The mosaic on the central pavement is by Joan Miró. The Casa Quadros, a Modernist building by Vilaseca (now a bank), is on the right. 45 min

Turn right past the flower market. Notice the ornate Modernist shop front of the Antiga Casa Figueras grocery shop on the left. Further on is the La Boqueria, a fascinating food market. Further on is the Palau Virreina, a notable building and cultural centre. At the old Jesuit church of Betlem, turn left into c/ Carme to reach the fine Gothic buildings of the Hospital de la Santa Creu, founded in the 11thC and now mostly used for cultural and educational purposes. Walk through quiet courtyards and gardens to exit on c/ de Hospital. Turn left to return to La Rambla. 45 min

Turn right, past the Gran Teatre del Liceu opera house. On the left a small passage opens into the Pl Reial, an attractive square. Opposite, on c/ Nou de la Rambla, note the Palau Güell by Gaudí. Carry on down La Rambla. This area was once the city's theatre-land. The modernist 'La Pitarra' monument commemorates the founder of modern Catalan drama. An alley leads to the Museu Cera (Wax Museum). The Palau Marc is an exhibition centre. La Rambla ends in the Pl Portal de la Pau (Gate of Peace) from which the monument to Columbus rises. On the right are the medieval shipyards (now Museu Marítim). In the port is a replica of Columbus's flagship *Santa Maria*, and *Las Golondrinas* which make short cruises across the harbour. M Drassanes. 30 min

Accidents and Breakdowns: The roads are patrolled regularly by the *Guardia Civil* and *Policía de Tráfico* who will help if you have an accident or breakdown, or you can summon assistance by phoning the operator (tel: 009, no coins required). It is best to join the AA or RAC at home who can provide information on driving rules and conditions in Spain, and advice on accident procedures before you leave on holiday. See **Driving, Emergencies**.

Accommodation: There is a wide choice of accommodation of all kinds and categories including hotels, hostels, tourist apartments, camp sites and holiday villages. Inevitably, many hotels in the Costa Brava are modern high-rise blocks erected to cater for the package holiday industry. They may not be all that attractive, but they are clean and have good facilities. During the high season, June-September, most three-star establishments are fully booked, and many close between October and March. Prices vary according to star rating (one to five, with Gran Lujo as extra-luxury) and season, and each room should display the applicable maximum charge inclusive of service and taxes. For something a little more stylish the Costa Brava has one Parador (high-quality state-run inn, usually sited in a historic building or beauty spot: Central Booking Office, Madrid. Tel: 435 9700) at Aiguablava, near Begur (see **TOWNS & VILLAGES 1, A-Z**) and there is the deluxe Hostal de la Gavina at S'Agaró (see **BUILDINGS 1, A-Z**). Villas and apartments are also popular choices for holidays or longer stays, and there's a wide range of locations, and varying quality and price. Most are Spanish and foreign-owned second homes and are made available to package holiday operators or can be rented through local agencies and service companies. Agencies and individuals also advertise in the holiday sections of British newspapers. A converted *masia* (farmhouse) in a rural setting is also an increasingly popular choice. Guest Houses (*Casas de Huéspedes*) and Inns (*Fondas*) offer the most basic accommodation. Local Tourist Offices can offer assistance with finding accommodation, and Spain's National Tourist Office in the UK can also provide information (see **Tourist Information**). See **Camping and Caravanning**.

Airports: Barcelona (El Prat), 4 km south of the city, handles interna-

tional flights and internal domestic services. It has all the usual amenities, including a tourist office. From 0630 to 2300 there is a train every 20 minutes to Sants, Barcelona's main railway station. Metered taxis are relatively inexpensive (they charge supplements for the 'airport' journey and for baggage). Girona Airport, 11 km south of the city (Exit 8 on autopista A 7), is a small regional airport which handles international charter flights from northern Europe. Amenities are limited and there is no tourist office nor any public transport between the airport and the town centre. Taxis are not metered but there are standard rates to different destinations.

Babysitters: Some hotels, apartment complexes and camping sites provide this service as well as daytime entertainment and care facilities. Others may arrange for professional baby-sitters on request. Make enquiries through your travel agent or tour operator. You can also enquire locally about *guarderías* (crèches).

Banks: See **Money**.

Banyoles: See **EXCURSION 1**, **TOWNS & VILLAGES 2**.

Beaches: The rugged coastline of the Costa Brava contains a variety of beaches from rocky inlets and small pebbly coves to wide stretches of golden sand. A few beaches remain relatively secluded and can only be reached on foot or by boat. Although all beaches are generally safe, sudden freak tidal conditions can make bathing dangerous, so be on guard. Pollution control has improved in recent years and the local authorities in resorts like Lloret and Tossa make great efforts to maintain cleanliness. Holiday-makers can help by dumping rubbish in the bins provided. See **RESORTS**.

Begur: The town sprawls around a hill with a 15thC castle which offers broad views north to Platja de Pals as far as l'Estartit and the Islas Medas. 2 km south are the local resorts of Platja de Fornells (site of the Parador - see **Accommodation**), Aiguablava and Sa Riera which nestle in a series of rocky coves (see **RESORTS 2**). See **TOWNS & VILLAGES 1**.

Besalú: This picturesque town, capital of the old county of Garrotxa, retains its medieval feel and in 1966 was declared a National Historic and Artistic Monument. Its angled bridge over the Riu Fluvià dates from the late 11thC, and the church of Sant Pere, the only remaining part of a monastery founded in 977, is an outstanding example of Catalan Romanesque (see **A-Z**). The Church of Sant Vicenç dates from the same period and has notable Lombard arches and a rose window. On a hill-top overlooking the town are the haunting Romanesque remains of the Church of Santa Maria. The Casa Llaudes has a lovely patio and the Hospital de Sant Julià an impressive portal. Porticoed buildings line the Plaça Mayor and c/ Tallaferro. Unique in Spain, and one of only three in Europe, is the *mikwà*, a Jewish ritual bath dating from the 12thC. See **EXCURSION 1, HISTORIC SITES, TOWNS & VILLAGES 2.**

Best Buys: Leather and suede clothing, footwear and accessories, in all price brackets, are recommended. Spanish fashion designers have

made their mark internationally and top name creations are found in smart boutiques of Girona (see **A-Z**), Platja d'Aro (see **A-Z**) and elsewhere. Other popular items are inexpensive Dalí (see **A-Z**) reproductions, or edible goods such as hand-made chocolates, canned anchovies, tinned olives and almonds. Local handicrafts are also widely available, although of variable quality. See **CRAFTS & CUSTOMS**.

Bicycle and Motorcycle Hire: These can be rented in all the resorts. Check that you are covered by your holiday insurance. The minimum age for hiring mopeds is 16; for motorcycles over 75cc it is 18. Crash helmets are only compulsory for the latter, but strongly recommended for both.

Bisbal, La: The capital of El Baix Empordà region and an important pottery producing centre, where you can watch the process of manufacture and buy the products in the town's numerous shops and handicraft centres (see **CRAFTS & CUSTOMS**). In the middle of the town is the Romanesque (see **A-Z**) palace which was once the seat of the Bishops of Girona. There is also a Baroque parish church in addition to some interesting 18thC houses. See **TOWNS & VILLAGES 1**.

Blanes: The southernmost resort on the Costa Brava, and despite its growth as a popular tourist centre still an important fishing port. Apart from the beaches, pleasure port and nightlife, the town's main attraction is the Marimurtra (Botanical Gardens) with more than 3000 species of Mediterranean plants, which also provides a superb panorama of the sweeping bay and coastline (open 0900-1800 daily). There are also the ruins of the 11thC Castell de Sant Joan on a hill to the north east which is worth climbing for the fine views over the town and beaches. See **MARKETS, RESORTS 1**.

Boat hire: Dinghies or pedaloes can be hired from beach-side operators during the high season; bigger craft from private owners or sailing clubs in some marinas. Fishermen may also hire out their boats (with crew) - enquire locally and agree prices in advance.

Bullfighting: Catalans have traditionally been less enthusiastic about this essentially Spanish entertainment than their cousins in the rest of the peninsula. Its aficionados regard the performance as an art form: a ritualized ballet where the danger heightens the intensity of the experience. The fate of the bull (*toro*), unfortunately, is always the same. The best idea if you wish to witness the spectacle is to go with one of the tour operators who often provide a guide who explains and then afterwards assesses the performance. Children under 15 are not admitted. There are bullfights every Sunday from the end of June to 15 September in Figueres, Girona, Lloret de Mar and San Feliu de Guíxols.

Buses: The easiest and least expensive means of exploring the area and a great way to meet the local people. A comprehensive network of scheduled services, *autobusos interurbans*, operated by SARFA, MAS, PUJOL and other companies, connect resort towns with each other and with Girona and Figueres. TEISA operates from Girona's railway station inland to places like Besalú, Banyoles, Olot and Ripoll. There are also services to Barcelona and to France, Holland, Belgium and Britain. For more information contact the local tourist office (see **Tourist Information**) or local bus station (*Estació de autobusos*).

Cadaqués: This picturesque town on the rugged Cap de Creus peninsula has attracted the attention of many notable painters and writers over the years, the most famous of whom was Dalí (see **A-Z**) who had a house at nearby Port Lligat (not open to the public). There is a popular town beach, and nearby coves of clear water reached on foot or by boat. It also has two notable museums (see **MUSEUMS 1**) and fine boutiques, restaurants and cafés. In July and August the town plays host to an international music festival (see **MUSIC & DANCE**). See **RESORTS 3**.

Calella de Palafrugell: See **RESORTS 2**, Palafrugell.

Camping and Caravanning: With over 100 official sites, there's a wide selection throughout the region and many have idyllic locations along the coast and inland. Some are mini-villages with good facilities for sports, entertainment, restaurants and shopping. There are four official categories from L (lux) to 1, 2 or 3. Book in advance for mid-June to mid-September. For a full list of sites contact the Tourist Office in Girona (see **Tourist Information**). Off-site camping is not encouraged and is never allowed on beaches, in mountain areas and along dry river beds. Tinder-dry vegetation is a high fire hazard in summer.

Car Hire: All the big international firms operate in the region, directly or with Spanish associates. Small local firms, whose leaflets can be picked up at hotels and tourist offices, usually have lower rates. Furthermore, many airlines offer 'fly-drive' schemes and many holiday operators have car hire offers. There are also firms which undertake bulk hiring so that they can pass on substantial discounts to tourists – look for their leaflets at the Spanish Tourist Office in your country. It's worth comparing all-inclusive costs as insurance and mileage charges can bump up the bill considerably. Note that insurance normally includes third-party and a bail bond (essential) but it is advisable to take, in addition, comprehensive insurance including a collision damage waiver. Remember that VAT is 12%. See **Accidents and Breakdowns**, **Driving**.

Catalunya: In 1979, this historically separate area, or nation with its own language and cultural distinctiveness, became one of Spain's 17 autonomous regions. It is divided into 38 *comarcas* (districts) within the four provinces of Barcelona, Girona, Tarragona and Lleida. The Catalan Parliament administers the region through its executive body, the *Generalitat*. Catalans also elect members to Spain's Parliament, the *Cortes*, and the central government controls defence, foreign policy and, in the opinion of many Catalans, still too many of Catalunya's internal affairs. See **Orientation**.

Catedral de Girona: The Cathedral of Santa Maria, which stands at the top of a Baroque stairway, was built between the 14thC and the 16thC. Much of the original Baroque facade was destroyed during the Civil War. The magnificent nave (50 m long and 23 m wide), one of the widest in existence, is flanked by 30 side chapels. In the adjoining chapterhouse is the Cathedral Museum (see **MUSEUMS 2**). In the Romanesque (see **A-Z**) cloister with its line of double columns, there is the five-floored tower of Charlemagne (Carlemany) from the 11thC, part of an earlier Romanesque church. Note the carvings of biblical scenes on capitals and friezes. See **BUILDINGS 2**, **EXCURSION 3**, **WALK 1**.

Chemists: See **Medical Treatment**.

Children: As is customary in Mediterranean countries, there is great fondness for and tolerance of children. They are made very welcome, almost anywhere and at any time. Beyond the beaches you will find other enjoyable distractions and opportunities for children to practise favourite sports, try something new and, hopefully, to learn from a different environment. Some resorts arrange summer events for children - enquire at local tourist offices on arrival (see **Tourist Information**). See CHILDREN, **Babysitters**.

Cigarettes and Tobacco: Sold in an *estanco* (or *tabacos*), many of which stock international brands. Spanish cigarettes are either *negro* (black tobacco) and strong like Ducados, or *rubio* (blond) and mild like Fortuna. Cigars from the Canaries are relatively inexpensive. Pipe tobaccos are mostly strong and coarse.

Cinema: Spain has an active and adventurous film industry. Most foreign films are dubbed. Showings in the original language with Spanish subtitles are advertised as 'v.o.'. First showing is usually at 1630, last at 2230.

Climate: Along the north-east Mediterranean coast the climate is generally mild and dry and gloriously sunny. The average temperatures are: summer 20°C-28°C; winter 12°C-14°C. Water temperatures are at their highest (23°C-25°C) in July, August and September. The wettest months are October and May. In winter the area is prone to the *tramontana*, a north-easterly wind which can send temperatures plummeting.

Complaints: Hotels, camp sites, restaurants and petrol stations have to keep *hojas de reclamación* (complaints forms in triplicate). If your complaint is about price, you must first pay the bill before requesting the forms. One copy is retained by you, another is sent to the tourism department of the regional government and the third is retained by the establishment against which the complaint is being made. This is a valuable consumer protection facility which should not be abused by using it for petty grievances. You could also contact the local tourist office, who may be willing to help with communication problems.

Consulates:

United Kingdom - Avinguda Diagonal 477, Edificio Torre de Barcelona
13th floor, Barcelona. Tel: (93) 322 31 69.
USA - Via Laietana 33, Barcelona. Tel: (93) 319 95 50.
Canada - Via Augusta 125, Barcelona. Tel: (93) 209 06 34.

Conversion Charts:

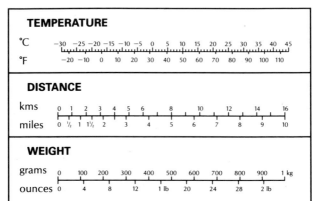

Cork: Once very important to the local economy, the cork industry on
which towns like Palafrugell and Sant Feliu de Guíxols thrived has
declined in the face of foreign competition and more attractive returns
from tourism. Cork trees remain a distinctive feature of the landscape.

Costa Brava: The name was coined in 1908 by the Catalan writer
Ferrán Agulló; whether he intended the name to mean 'wild' or 'dangerous' is unclear, but it is now used for the 214 km of coastline featuring rugged cliffs, rocky coves, sandy beaches and forests stretching
from Blanes (see **RESORTS 1**, **A-Z**) in the south to the Franco/Spanish
town of Portbou (see **RESORTS 3**) in the north.

Costa Maresme: Often included as part of the Costa Dourada, the 'marsh coast' extends north from Barcelona to meet the Costa Brava. It has good beaches, and its resorts such as Canet de Mar offer moderately-priced accommodation making them popular with Spanish families. Arenys de Mar is a large sailing centre, and Mataro and Premia de Mar are famous for their carnations, Spain's national flower. Much of the good-quality fruit, vegetables and salads come from this fertile stretch of coastal plain.

Courtesies: Catalans are generally quieter in public and more circumspect about expressing emotions than other Spaniards. Two important expressions are *por favor* (please) and *gracias* (thank you). Going into a room, shop, elevator, or when formally meeting people, the greeting is *buenos días* (good day) or *buenas tardes* (afternoon and evening). Leaving, it's *adiós* or *buenas noches* (goodnight). A much used phrase is *de res* (you're welcome).

Crime: Violent assaults are rare and, considering the large influx of tourists each summer, crime figures are relatively low. However, care lessness about personal security makes life easy for petty criminals,

local or foreign. Deposit valuables in the hotel or apartment safe; ensure that your hotel room, apartment or villa is securely locked when you leave; carry the least possible amount of cash; don't flash cash around when leaving a bank; carry handbags and cameras on the off-street side; don't leave anything in sight in a car; use licensed taxis at night. If you have been the victim of a crime, try to find witnesses and report the incident to the police immediately. Keep a copy of your statement for insurance purposes. See **Emergencies**, **Police**.

Customs:

Duty Paid Into:	Cigarettes	or	Cigars	or	Tobacco	Spirits	Wine
E.E.C.	300		75		400 g	1.5 l	5 l
U.K.	300		75		400 g	1.5 l	5 l

Dalí, Salvador (1904-89): Born in Figueres (see TOWNS & VILLAGES 2). After a conventional art training at Madrid's School of Fine Arts he joined the Parisian milieu of the Surrealists Breton and Eluard. With the earliest and best of his Surrealist works, like *The Persistence of Memory* (1931) with its melting watches, and in his cinematic collaboration with Luis Buñuel - *Un Chien Andalou* (1929) and *L'Age d'Or* (1930) - he broke new ground, showing that dreams and fantasies could be the vivid subjects of pictorial and cinematic art rather than just hidden stimuli for artistic expression. In the thirties he reached the high point of his international critical acclaim, but as his fame increased so the respect of his Surrealist colleagues waned, especially after his support for Franco, and he was expelled from the movement. In later years an exceptional talent for self-publicity made him the century's first art pop star. He is buried in the Figueres museum. See EXCURSION 1, MUSEUMS 1.

Dentists: see **Medical Treatment**.

Disabled: Toilet facilities are limited, although there are increasing efforts to provide for the disabled, for example in some of Girona's museums and new accommodation complexes. Be sure to inform travel agents or holiday operators of specific needs before booking.

Drinks: *Agua potable* (tap water) is quite safe although you may have some unwanted effects simply because your system is not used to it. It's best to stick to bottled mineral water (*agua mineral*). *Té* (tea) is usually served with a slice of lemon, and *Infusión de manzanilla* is refreshing camomile tea. *Horchata* is a cool, refreshing drink made from ground nuts. *Granizado* is iced, fresh fruit juice. Coffee (*café*) comes either black (*solo*) or with milk (*con leche*). Various qualities of local and imported beer (*cerveza*) are available. *Una caña* (draught beer) is usually lower priced. *Sangría* is a mixture of ice, soda water, red wine, brandy, fruit and juices, whose strength depends on the individual recipe. Sherry (*Jerez*) is either pale dry (*fino*), medium (*amontillado*), or heavier and sweeter (*oloroso*). Brandies (*coñacs*) vary from the rough to fine (10 year or older reservas). Liqueurs, vermouths and dessert wines are also made locally. *Cremat*, a flamed, cinnamon spiced mix of coffee, rum and liqueur, is a Costa Brava speciality. See **Wines**.

Driving: When driving in Spain you will need your passport, current driving licence (international or EC), vehicle registration document, international insurance certificate (green card) and bail bond (usually issued with green card or covered by car hire agreement document) and a red warning triangle (if you're going on motorways). Drive on the right and overtake on the left. Give way to traffic coming from the right, especially at roundabouts, unless it's clearly marked that your road has priority. Never cross a solid white line to overtake or turn left. Always use indicators and horn when overtaking. Speed limits are 60 kph on most urban roads; 90 kph on other roads where indicated; 100 kph on main roads; 120 kph on motorways. Belts must be worn in front seats outside urban areas. No hooting in urban areas unless in an emergency. Don't drink and drive (permitted maximum is 0.8 g alcohol per 1000

cc). Penalties for motoring offences can be severe and include prison terms, and fines must be paid on the spot. Parking prohibitions are usually clearly marked by painted kerbstones and signs. Some petrol stations close on Sundays and holidays.

Drugs: The Spanish authorities have recently introduced a strict policy of prosecuting those found in possession of or dealing in illegal drugs.

Eating Places: Most of the big tourist hotels have unadventurous, bland international menus. If you want to play safe when eating out you're sure to find expatriate-owned restaurants in the resorts to suit you. Fast-food hamburger, pizza and chicken and chips take-aways are also plentiful. There are also plenty of more memorable gastronomic and cultural experiences awaiting those who venture beyond these places to local *bodegas* (liquor shops), *tabernas*, bars and cafés, serving alcoholic drinks and tasty appetizers called *tapas* (see **A-Z**) and to restaurants serving traditional cuisine, other Spanish regional styles, or the new wave Mediterranean cooking.

The official grading of restaurants, 1-5 forks, reflects the standard of facilities, not that of the cooking. Meal times: breakfast until 1100; lunch 1300-1500; dinner from 2030 (most popular tourist spots open earlier). See **RESTAURANTS**, **Food**.

Electricity: 220 or 225 volt, although older buildings may still use 125 volt supply, so be sure to check before you use an appliance. Plugs are round pin, two point, so you will need a plug adaptor.

Emergencies: If you are in or near urban areas, telephone 091 for the Policia Nacional (or 20 45 26 - Girona city). In rural areas call the Guardia Civil on 20 11 00 (or Traffic Section on 20 13 81). Concentrate on giving your location, the nature of the emergency and stating what other services may be required. See **Police**.

Empúries: In the 6thC BC the site was originally an island on which the Greeks built a port (Palaeopolis), and they later built another port on the mainland (Neapolis). By the 1stC BC the Romans had conquered and extended the settlement, calling it Emporiae. The local town L'Escala (see **RESORTS 3, A-Z**) was founded in the 17thC using building stones from the ruins. The main excavations concentrated on Neapolis, and the major find was a statue of Asclepius, the Greek god of medicine (the original is now in Barcelona's Archeological Museum). On the right of the entrance gate are the remains of a temple of the sun god Zeus Sarapis. On the left of the entrance gate was a sacred precinct plus watchtower and water cisterns. On the seaward side of the present museum are: outlines of the Agora, or town centre; the Stoa, a covered market place; and an early Christian basilica. The extensive Roman town has been only partially excavated. Most prominent are two houses showing their layout and mosaics, as well as outlines of a rectangular forum and the amphitheatre. The museum (Museo Monográfico) contains exhibits illustrating the archeological history of the site, and includes artefacts and model reconstructions
See **EXCURSION 1, HISTORIC SITES**.

Escala, L': A small fishing port and holiday resort. The old quarter of El Passeig has attractive streets with balconied houses and shops. To the south is the Platja dels Riells (often dirty), the leisure and fishing port, and popular Cala Montgó. Northwards, pines shelter pleasant beaches along the road to the hamlet of Sant Martí d'Empúries, close to the site of Empúries (see **EXCURSION 1, HISTORIC SITES, A-Z**). See **RESORTS 3**.

Estartit L': A mostly modern town and holiday resort with a large pleasure harbour. The coastline is a mixture of rocky grottoes (great for snorkelling and diving) and long sandy beaches with holiday apart-, ments and tower blocks. See **RESORTS 2**.

Events: During the summer hardly a day passes without a fiesta somewhere in the region. Whether the inspiration be pagan, Christian or plainly commercial, they usually climax with a loosening of inhibitions and general merrymaking in which visitors are welcome to join. Many include dancing of *sardanes* (see **A-Z**), performances of *havaneres* (see **A-Z**) and colourful parades.

March - Easter observations, large procession in Girona and in towns throughout the region. *April* - Book Fair in Barcelona; Feast day of Catalunya's patron, Sant Jordi (23rd). *May* - Figueres Town Festival (first week); Ripoll Town Fair; Corpus Christi: streets of Tossa, Arbúcies and elsewhere are strewn with flowers. *June* - Sant Joan's day (24th) coincides with the summer solstice and is celebrated with bonfires and fireworks. *July* - Cadaqués International Music Festival (until Aug.). *August* - La Bisbal Town Festival; Peratallada Festa Major; Roses Festa Major. *September* - Celebrations everywhere on Catalunya's National Day (11th); Besalú Festa Major; Cadaqués Festival; Figueres International Music Festival in Vilabertran; Tossa *sardana* competition.

For details of all fiestas contact tourist offices (see **Tourist Information**).

Figueres: A small town 35 km north of Girona. Its biggest attraction is the Teatre-Museu Dalí (see **MUSEUMS 1**). See **EXCURSION 1**, **TOWNS & VILLAGES 2**.

Fishing: Brightly-coloured fishing boats decorate many beaches. Some may rot there for it becomes increasingly difficult to make a living with small boats as inshore waters yield less and less. Bigger boats go out further and return around five in the afternoon to have their varied catches sold at the lively, colourful auctions of Blanes and Palamós (see **MARKETS**). If you fancy sea fishing, enquire at the local tourist office (see **Tourist Information**) about the best spots for rock fishing or boat and tackle hire. Most resorts have a bait shop. You might catch sole,

sea bass, denton, *dorado* or sea bream. Inland, there are trout, barbel, carp, tench and pike. For more information and the essential licence apply to ICONA, Av Sant Francesc 29, Girona (Tel: 20 09 87).

Flamenco: Four separate talents are expressed in a full performance of this folk dance from Andalucía: *cante* (singing), *baile* (dancing), *toque* (guitar playing) and *jaleo* (rhythmic clapping and footwork). The best performers are said to have *duende*, an inexplicable attribute. *Flamenco jondo* is profound and melancholy, and expresses the deepest emotions. *Flamenco chico*, lighter and livelier, is more about sensuous love and sadnesses overcome. Commercial performances usually consist of a popularized mix of the two. See NIGHTLIFE.

Food: Catalan cuisine is renowned throughout Spain for its quality and variety. For breakfast there are *pastissos* - croissants and brioches. A favourite snack or starter is *pa amb tomàquet*, bread rubbed with fresh tomato, seasoned with salt and olive oil, served plain or as the base for an open sandwich, like *pernil de Pirineu*, which uses mountain ham. *Sopas* (soups) can be filling, such as *escudella de pagès*, vegetables in meat stock; lighter is *sopa d'alls i menta*, with garlic and mint. Different *amanidas* (salads) too can often be meals by themselves. *Escalivada*, grilled red pepper and aubergine with an olive oil dressing, is a favourite starter. *Pastes* (pastas) and *arros* (rice) are both important in Catalan cuisine, as is *peix* (fish) either simply grilled, *a la planxa*, or in a dish like *sarsuela*, assorted fish boiled with tomatoes, peppers and peas. Delicious too is *bacallà amb panses i pinyons*, cod with raisins and pine nuts. *Llagosta i pollastre*, a light stew of lobster and chicken, is a delicious combination. *Carn* (meat) can be good-quality cuts simply charcoal grilled, or more unusual dishes like *ánec amb peres*, duck with pears, and *conill amb cargols*, rabbit with snails. As a nation with a very sweet tooth, the Catalans make lots of light, tempting pastries and tarts. And their *crema catalana* of beaten eggs, milk, sugar and cinnamon below a caramel crust is always scrumptious. See **Tapas**.

Gaudí, Antoni (1852-1926): Spain's most famous architect and exponent of Catalan *Modernisme*. His early work was influenced by Mudéjar (see **A-Z**), Baroque and Gothic tradition, but evolved into an unclassifiable style marked by freedom of form, extravagant colour and texture, and use of organic motifs. His most famous building is the unfinished Temple de la Sagrada Família in Barcelona to which he devoted much of his life. See **EXCURSION 2**.

Girona: The capital of Girona province is a historic town with notable churches, museums and a Gothic cathedral. It is well worth a day trip inland from the coast. See **EXCURSION 3**, **TOWNS & VILLAGES 1**, **WALK 1 & 2**.

Golf: See **SPORTS**.

Guides: Contact local tourist offices or write to Patronat de Turisme Costa Brava Girona, Pl Marquès de Camps 17, 17001 Girona.

Hairdressers: In Spanish *peluquería*, they are plentiful, but prices vary greatly.

Havaneres: Traditional songs sung by sailors and fishermen, which were brought back by emigrants to Cuba in the 19thC who later returned home. Now it is a principal form of folk expression along the coast, especially in bars in Llafranc (see **RESORTS 2**) and L'Escala (see **RESORTS 3, A-Z**). They are taken very seriously by some, but others use the occasion as an excuse to enjoy *cremat* (see **Drinks**). See **Events**.

Horse Riding: For beginners or experienced riders there are many opportunities for excursions through a variety of lovely countryside. There is at least one Club Hipic in or near the following towns: Blanes, Lloret de Mar, Sant Feliu de Guíxols, Platja d'Aro, Calonge, Palafrugell, Begur, Pals, L'Estartit, L'Escala, Castelló d'Empúries, Roses, Girona, Banyoles, Puigcerdà. Local tourist offices have details. See **SPORTS**.

Language: Castilian is Spain's official language, but Catalans have their own distinct language which is accorded equal status, and is also spoken (with various dialects) in Valencia, the Balearic Islands, Andorra and the eastern French Pyrenees. Since the death of Franco, Catalan language and literature has flourished as a proud expression of regional autonomy from Castilian and Madrid-centred culture and politics.

Laundries: Hotels have laundry and dry cleaning services. A *lavandería* (laundry) or *tintorería* (dry cleaner) is likely to be cheaper. They

usually charge by weight and need a minimum of 24 hours. A few are self-service.

Lloret de Mar: The largest and most popular resort on the coast has a long, broad beach with clean, coarse sand backed by a palm-shaded promenade; beyond are the hotel and apartment blocks and brash commercial development which has transformed this once quiet fishing village. It provides an excellent choice of nightlife, with plenty of bars, discos, nightclubs and casinos (see **NIGHTLIFE**). There are good beaches to the south - Fanals, Boadella and Santa Cristina. See **RESORTS 1**.

Lost Property: If you lose anything inform your hotel receptionist or a person in charge wherever you are staying, and they may contact the local lost property office (usually the town hall) for you. If the loss is serious, report it to the police and get a copy of your statement. Promptly advise credit card companies, issuers of traveller's cheques and, if your passport is lost, your consulate (see **A-Z**). See **Police**.

Medical Treatment: It is unwise to leave home without travel insurance providing accident and medical cover. Take a copy of the policy with you and make a separate note of its details and any emergency telephone numbers. Your hotel, or other place of accommodation, will assist in calling a doctor or making an appointment with doctors or dentists. Tourist offices (see **Tourist Information**) have lists of practitioners. You will be required to pay for each visit or consultation. Emergency cases are usually accepted at both public and private clinics or hospitals. Unless you have obtained a card entitling you to Spanish public health services, you will be charged for these services in the same way as by private clinics. On presentation of your insurance policy, practitioners and clinics may accept waiting for payment of large bills from the insurers. Chemists (*farmacias*) have green cross signs. Prescription medicines are relatively inexpensive, and a notice on the door will give the address of the nearest chemist open after normal hours. Keep all receipts for subsequent submission to your insurers.

Money: The peseta (pta) is Spain's monetary unit. Notes: 10,000,

5000, 2000, 1000, 500, 200, 100 (going out of circulation). Coins: 500, 200, 100, 50, 25, 10, 5, 1. Banks offer the best exchange rate, and remember that you need your passport for any transaction. The major international credit cards are widely accepted, as are traveller's cheques in any west European currency or US dollars and Eurocheques supported by a valid card. Check with your credit or charge card company at which Spanish cash dispensers you can use your card and PIN. *Caixa* is Catalan for Savings Bank and many branches offer exchange facilities.

Montserrat: Site of the famous monastery set in spectacular mountain scenery which is one of Spain's greatest sights. See **EXCURSION 4**.

Moors: The collective word for Arabs, Berbers and other Moslems who invaded Spain from North Africa in 711 and rapidly gained control of the peninsula. They did not stay long in the north-eastern part as they were pushed back by Charlemagne, King of the Franks, and by 800 the area of today's Girona province was part of a relatively secure buffer zone between Moslem and Christian.

Mudéjar: A Moslem under Christian rule. The term is also used to describe the architectural style combining Christian and Moorish elements, which was prevalent in the 13th-16thCs.

Music: There are various music festivals held during the summer in towns throughout the region (see **MUSIC & DANCE**, **Events**). For jazz, rock and pop performances, check local listings. Major events are staged·in Girona's bullring. See **Flamenco**, **Havaneres**, **Sardana**.

Newspapers: Most international newspapers and magazines in English are widely available, and the British quality press and tabloids are available on their day of publication, although they are more expensive than at home. The *Iberian Daily Sun* briefly covers some Spanish and international news in English.

Olot: See **TOWNS & VILLAGES 3**.

Olympics 1992: The Summer Olympics of 1992 are scheduled to start in Barcelona on 25 July, the feast day of St James (Jaume), Spain's patron saint. Some of the world's best known architects are involved in a huge programme of building and urban improvement which is now under way. The Olympic Ring on Montjuïc will be the main centre of activity. Competitors will stay in the Olympic Village, designed by the Catalan architect, Oriol Bohigas, on a site between Parc Ciutadella and the sea. The Olympic Flame will arrive in Spain at Empúries. Rowing events will be held on the lake at Banyoles. See **EXCURSION 1 & 2**.

Opening Times: In general:
Shops - 0930-1330, 1630-2000 Mon.-Fri., 0930-1400 Sat.
Department Stores - 1000-2000 Mon.-Sat.
Business Offices - 0900-1400, 1630-1900 Mon.-Fri.
Government Offices - 1100-1300 Mon.-Fri. (for public business).
Banks - 0900-1400 Mon.-Fri., 0930-1300 Sat.
Post Offices - 0900-1300 Mon.-Fri. (main ones may also open 1700-1900), 0900-1400 Sat.

Orientation: Girona, the north-eastern province of Catalunya (see **A-Z**), has an area of 5886 km² and incorporates the regions of L'Alt Empordà, El Baix Empordà and La Selva. It is bordered to the west and south by the Provinces of Lleida and Barcelona respectively. The eastern seaboard constitutes the Costa Brava (see **A-Z**). Girona city (see **EXCURSION 3**, **TOWNS & VILLAGES 1**, **WALK 1 & 2**, **A-Z**) is the provincial capital. It is on the north/south A 7 toll motorway (*autopista*), 60 km from the French border and 100 km from Barcelona (see **EXCURSION 2**).

Palafrugell: The local town for the neighbouring beach resorts of Calella de Palafrugell, Llafranc and Tamariu (see **RESORTS 2**). Nearby is the Ermita de San Sebastián which has a viewing platform and restaurant offering wonderful views over the steep cliffs and along the rugged coastline.

Palamós: Commercial port and holiday resort, with a beach of fine sand. One of its main attractions is the afternoon fish market (see **MAR-**

KETS). It has a pleasure harbour and is the location for international regattas. The Gothic Church of Santa Maria dominates the old town, and to the north are two good beaches, Platja de la Fosca and the Platja del Castell. See **RESORTS 1**.

Pals: A medieval village with a Romanesque parish church and 10thC town walls (see **HISTORIC SITES**). The Platja de Pals (see **RESORTS 2**) is a wide stretch of beach at the mouth of the River Ter with large tourist developments. See **TOWNS & VILLAGES 1**.

Passports and Customs: Visitors holding a valid passport of an EC country, the United States or Canada do not require a visa to enter Spain. British Visitors' Passports are also accepted. Australian, New Zealand, South African, Japanese and some other passport holders have to obtain a visa from a Spanish Consulate.

Peralada: A small town 6 km north east of Figueres worth visiting for its attractive Castillo originally built between the 14th and 17thCs and

heavily restored in the 19thC. Originally owned by the Rocaberti family, the counts of Peralada, it combines Gothic and Renaissance elements. Inside is a casino, restaurant, theatre, an extensive library and museum (1000-1200, 1630-1830 Mon.-Sat., 1000-1200 Sun.).

Peratallada: See HISTORIC SITES, TOWNS & VILLAGES 1.

Photography: All makes and sizes of film are available in the resorts. Do not attempt to photograph policemen, military personnel or installations. Flash photography is not permitted in some churches, museums, etc. Film development and printing is generally more expensive in Spain than in other European countries, but many resorts have fast processing outlets which charge reasonable prices.

Platja d'Aro: One of the most popular resorts on the Costa Brava. Its wide beach of coarse sand and shingle stretches for 1 km, backed by hotels and apartment blocks. There is a good selection of shops, cafés, bars, restaurants (see RESTAURANTS 2) and nightspots (see NIGHTLIFE). Castell d'Aro, a quiet village, is 3 km to the west. See RESORTS 1,

Police: The *Policía Nacional* are the tough, smart-looking men and women in blue uniforms and berets who walk the streets in twos and patrol in white or tan vehicles. Report any crime to them and make a formal statement at their *comisaría*. The *Policía Municipal* (blue uniforms, white or blue cars) deal mainly with the city's traffic and enforcing municipal regulations. You'll see the *Guardia Civil* (green uniforms and tricorn hats) at immigration and customs posts and patrolling roads and rural areas. Catalunya's own police force, *Mossos d'Esquadra* (dark blue uniforms, red cap bands), have a role somewhere between the other branches. See **Emergencies**.

Post Offices: Look for *Correos*. Mail to be collected must be addressed *'lista de correos'* or *'poste restante'*. Take your passport as identification for collections. A postcard is a *tarjeta postal*. Stamps (*sellos*) can also be bought from your hotel or tobacconists (*estancos*). Mail boxes (*buzones*) are yellow with red stripes. See **Opening Times**.

Public Holidays: Public Holidays are celebrated on the following days: 1 Jan., 6 Jan., 19 Mar., 1 May, 25 July, 15 Aug., 12 Oct., 1 Nov., 8 Dec., 25 Dec. and on the variable feast days of Good Friday, Easter Monday and Corpus Christi. Businesses and banks also close on local fiesta days (see **Events**).

Public Toilets: These are scarce, and if there is an attendant a small tip is customary. Owners of bars, cafés and other eating places do not usually object to use of their facilities by non-customers.

Radio and TV: The Ràdio Associació de Catalunya (105 MHz) and Catalunya Ràdio (88.4 MHz) broadcast news in English at 1030 Mon.-Fri. during July and August. Many hotels are equipped with satellite TV dishes to pick up various British and European stations, including Channel 10, Sky and Super.

Railways: Girona and Figueres are principal stops on the main Barcelona to Perpignan line (via Portbou). There are six to eight trains both ways daily. Blanes is on the coastal line from Barcelona which links with the main line at Maçanet de la Selva. There are services from Blanes to Costa Maresme resorts and Barcelona every 30 minutes in summer and hourly during the rest of year; and to Girona every two hours. For further information contact Estació RENFE Girona, tel: 20 70 93 or 20 32 87.

Religious Services: Tourist offices (see **Tourist Information**) can provide information about Catalan, Castilian or foreign language services in local Catholic churches. Your consulate (see **A-Z**) may advise about other denomination services in Barcelona.

Restaurants: Price indications are - Budget, most main courses under 1200ptas; Moderate, under 2000ptas; Expensive, over 3000ptas. Grading of restaurants, one to five forks, reflects standard of facilities, not necessarily of cooking or service. See **RESTAURANTS**, **Eating Places**.

Ripoll: A small industrial town 86 km north west of Girona (see **EXCURSION 3**, **TOWNS & VILLAGES 1**, **WALK 1 & 2**, **A-Z**) deep in the interior of the province. It is the site of the Benedictine Monastery of Santa Maria (see **BUILDINGS 2**, **MUSEUMS 2**, **A-Z**), founded in the 9thC by Wilfred the Hairy, first Count of Barcelona.

Romanesque: An artistic style, broadly shared throughout western Europe, which came to Catalunya (see **A-Z**) earlier than the rest of Spain (c. 10thC). Girona province is very well endowed with surviving buildings, mostly churches. The doorway and cloister of Ripoll's Santa Maria monastery are outstanding examples (see **BUILDINGS 2**, **MUSEUMS 2**, **A-Z**). Buildings from the period are restrained and utilitarian with didactic carvings on capitals and doorways providing decorative relief. Square or octagonal towers are prominent features. Boldly-coloured frescoes and paintings on wooden panels adorn the churches' stark interiors. The style was linear in the Byzantine tradition and the purpose was to inform and instruct an illiterate populace. Wood carving too showed Byzantine influence - rigid postures, clothes and hair arranged decoratively rather than realistically.

Romans: In 218 BC, during the Second Punic War between Rome and Carthage, the Roman general Scipio landed at what is now Empúries (see **EXCURSION 1**, **HISTORIC SITES**, **A-Z**) and colonization of the peninsula began. The area of today's Catalunya (see **A-Z**) formed part of the imperial province of Tarraconensis whose capital was Terraco (Tarragona). Barcino (Barcelona) and Gerunda (Girona) were important administrative centres. The Forca street in Girona formed part of the great Via Augusta. In 49 BC Caesar ordered the construction of a large new town at Empúries in which to settle his army veterans. As the Roman empire crumbled in the late 4thC, Vandals and other raiding tribes appeared. Then the Visigoths, converts to Byzantine Christianity, took over as rulers of the peninsula and between 531-48 Barcino was their capital.

Roses: A fishing port and popular holiday resort. Villa and apartment complexes spread behind the good beaches of del Rastell, Salatar and Santa Margarida (a holiday complex built around a system of canals) where most of the big hotels are also located. At the opposite (eastern) side of the bay, white villas and apartment blocks speckle the hill of Puig Rom which rises above the port. Further east, Canyelles (Petites and Grosses) and Montjoi are three coves with pleasant beaches, hotels and other amenities. More villas are scattered among the hills behind the town and along the roads to Cadaqués (see **RESORTS 3**, **A-Z**) and Figueres (see **EXCURSION 1**, **TOWNS & VILLAGES 2**, **A-Z**). The rather characterless town centre has the ruins of a fort, La Ciutadella. See **RESORTS 3**.

S'Agaró: A relatively modern development begun by the Ensesas family in 1923 and planned to complement the natural surroundings. It is one of Spain's most exclusive and attractive residential areas, with splendid villas and the de luxe Hostal La Gavina. See **BUILDINGS 1**.

Sailing and Water Sports: Most of the 18 marinas along the coast have short-term berthing and service facilities for visiting craft. Regattas are held throughout the year, although most are in summer. Boats and yachts can be chartered locally. Lessons in dinghy sailing, water-skiing and windsurfing are available in pleasure ports and on many beaches. The lake of Banyoles (see **EXCURSION 1**, **TOWNS & VILLAGES 2**) is Spain's premier inland water sports location. For more information contact the local tourist office or the individual resort's *Club Nàutic* or *Club de Vela*.

Sant Feliu de Guíxols: Self-styled 'Capital of the Costa Brava', this small port is one of the quieter resorts, and has an air of gentility and elegance. The narrow beach is backed by shady parks and the fine Passeig del Mar and dels Guíxols with casinos, good shops and restaurants. From the beach a road leads to the Hermitage de Sant Elm and the mirador from which there are superb views over the town and along the coast to Tossa (see **RESORTS 1**, **A-Z**). There is an interesting local museum (see **MUSEUMS 1**), and notable architectural features include the ruins of the medieval monastery and church including the 11thC Porta Ferrada and nearby Arc de Sant Benet, and several Modernist buildings (see **BUILDINGS 1**). See **RESORTS 1**.

Sant Pere de Rodes: The ruins of a former Benedictine Monastery consecrated in 1022 and one of the best examples of Catalan Romanesque (see **A-Z**) design. Sacked by Napoleon's troops in 1798 and abandoned. See **HISTORIC SITES**.

Santa Maria de Ripoll: A monastery, first founded in 589 and generously endowed with a new church in 888 by Count Wilfred the Hairy, first Count of Barcelona. It was an important centre of scholarship under its abbot Oliba from 1008 to 1046. The library and school maintained the study of subjects neglected elsewhere in the Christian world. Abbot Oliba's grand church was consecrated in 1032. Only the extraordinary, iconographic portal remains, now protected within a glazed porch. Its panels of intricate carvings taught people about the glory of God. The main building was sacked in 1835 and the restoration which started in 1886 strove to recreate the original. Of the beautiful cloister only the lower gallery joined to the church is of the original 12thC structure. See **BUILDINGS 2**.

Sardana: Catalunya's prim and sedate national dance has its roots in Girona province and probably stems from a more lively harvest dance of ancient times. On Sundays and high *festa* days, dancers form a circle - anyone and any number can usually join in - link hands at shoulder height and with neat footwork go through an intricate sequence of steps and pauses to the accompaniment of *la cobla*, an eleven-piece band of wind instruments and double bass. See **Events**.

Spas: The Romans made good use of the curative waters from hot mineral springs at Caldeas de Malavella, 15 km south of Girona. There are two moderately-priced three-star hotels. Both offer professional hydrotherapy, inhalations and other health and beauty treatments. The waters are especially good for respiratory, digestive and circulatory ailments. Balneario Prats (tel: 47 00 51), where Rosa Quintana quickly makes guests very welcome and relaxed, has the most charm and attracts a younger crowd, especially at weekends.

Balneario Vichy Catalan (tel: 47 00 00) is larger and grander. At Santa Coloma de Farners the Balneario Termes Orion (tel: 84 00 65) is more modest and its waters are recommended for treatment of rheumatism and nervous disorders.

Sport: There's squash, table tennis, golf, scuba-diving, flying, hang-gliding, billiards and bowling. Some hotel or apartment complexes and campsites arrange sports competitions. Spectator events include football, basketball, pelota and cycling. Tourist offices can provide fuller information and addresses of local sports federations. See **SPORTS, Fishing, Horse Riding, Sailing and Water Sports, Tennis**.

Tapas: Many bars serve these tempting appetizers, ranging from olives, nuts or crisps to small and tasty portions of meats, seafood, omelettes, salads or vegetables at varying prices. All are temptingly displayed on the counter so you can indicate what you want. Some are served hot. *Raciones* are larger portions.

Taxis: Inexpensive by international comparison. They are available for hire when showing a *libre* sign on the windscreen and a small green light on the roof. A list of supplements which may be added to the metered fare is shown in the cab. Fares are higher after 2100 and at weekends. Taxis without meters charge officially-fixed fares for some journeys, and for others it may be necessary to negotiate a fare. It is always wise to get an idea in advance of what your journey is going to cost, especially for longer trips.

Telephones: Hotels charge heavily for international calls. The area code is 972. Cheap rate is from 2200-0800. Coin-operated booths require 5 (local calls only), 25, 50 or 100ptas coins. Place coins in the sloping groove at the top of the coin box. Lift the receiver, check for dial tone, then dial. Coins will drop into the box as needed. Codes for Spanish provinces and other countries are given in the booths. For local calls dial the number only. For international calls, after the dialling tone, dial 07, wait for the second dialling tone, then dial the country code plus area code (exclude initial 0) plus number. At the Telefónica cabins which are operated in many resorts during the season payment is easier (after the call) and assistance is available. Telex and Fax: available from some hotels and from business services bureaux in some towns. Telegram: by telephone on 20 20 00 and at Post Offices.

Tennis: Finding courts and people to play with should be easy. Besides those of tennis clubs, there are courts at many hotels, apartments and camp sites, as well as some municipal sports facilities. Professional tuition is offered at some. See **SPORTS**.

Time differences: Same time as western Europe: one hour ahead of GMT and 6-12 hours ahead of the USA.

Tipping: Although it may not be shown separately, a service charge is included on hotel and restaurant bills. However, it is still the practice to leave around 5-10% in restaurants and to tip hotel staff for special services. At the bar, leave a token tip of 5-10% for table service. Taxi drivers, hairdressers and tour guides usually get around 10%. Lavatory attendants, doormen, shoeshines and car parking attendants - 25, 50 or 100ptas.

Tossa de Mar: Popular resort on a horseshoe bay with a wide sweep of beach. The picturesque Old Town (Vila Vella - see **HISTORIC SITES**) preserves its narrow, winding medieval streets and is surrounded by 12thC walls. The area once attracted various artists and writers, including the painter Marc Chagall who visited the town in 1933; one of his works is in the local museum (see **MUSEUMS 1**) along with a variety of local archeological finds. See **RESORTS 1**.

Tourist Information:
In the UK: Spanish National Tourist Office, 57 St James's St, London
SW1, tel: (01) 499 0901.
Girona: The regional tourist office is Oficina de Turisme de Girona,
Ciutadans 12, tel: (972) 20 16 94 (open 0900-1400, 1500-1800 Mon.-
Sat., 0900-1400 Sun.); the local office is Plaça del Vi 1, tel: (972) 20 26
79 (open 0800-2000 Mon.-Sat.). There is also an office at the main rail-
way station, tel: (972) 21 62 86.
For other resorts, towns and villages in the region the general opening
times are 1000-1300, 1700-1900 Mon.-Sat.

Ullastret: Site of Poblat Ibèric, excavations of an Iberian settlement
on an earlier Iron Age site, in an attractive parkland setting. The town
probably dates from the 7thC BC, but economic competition from the
Greek town of Emporion (see **Empúries**) to the north led to the aban-
donment of the site in the 2ndC BC. Excavations of the area only began
in 1947 and are still continuing. Within the remains of the fortified
walls are a series of streets, store rooms and cisterns. The museum contains weapons and domestic and agricultural implements from the
excavations. See **HISTORIC SITES**.

Vic: An old cathedral town 60 km north of Barcelona. The
Neoclassical cathedral was built on the site of a Romanesque (see **A-Z**)
church, and was reconstructed after damage during the Civil War.
Inside are a series of impressive frescoes by the Catalan artist Josep
Maria Sert, and the main altarpiece is sculpted from alabaster and dates
from the 15thC. Also notable is the Baroque silver tomb of St Bernat
Calbó. The Museu Episcopal contains important works of Romanesque
art, pre-Christian artefacts, clerical garb and other religious items
(1000-1300, 1600-1900 Mon.-Fri., 1000-1300 Sun. and hols.).

Walks: Some Tourist Information Offices (see **A-Z**) have printed sug-
gestions for seashore and country walks and a few organize walking
excursions. Some paths are obvious, others are marked. Isolated *calas*
and *ermitas* (hermitages) are the usual destinations along the coast.
Inland, there are superb areas for gentle or more arduous hikes in the

Les Guilleries, Montseny, Banyoles, Santa Pau/Olot and La Cerdanya districts. If you want to go on a trek, never walk alone, don't be too ambitious, wear sensible shoes and a hat, and carry an item of warmer clothing, water and a snack.

Wine: *Vino* (or *vi* in Catalan) is the national drink - *tinto* (red), *blanco* (white) or *rosado* (rosé). Catalunya (see **A-Z**) has five *denominaciones de origen* (D.O.), officially demarcated and controlled wine growing areas, of which Penedés, southwest of Barcelona, is the best known. Its whites are fresh, fruity and aromatic, the reds smooth and light. It also produces superb *cavas*, sparkling wines made by the champagne method, mainly at Sadurni d'Anoia. The D.O. of Ampurdán-Costa Brava is relatively small and its bodegas are updating their production methods. Rosés, quite dark and aromatic, have been its hallmark, while its heavy reds and indifferent whites have mostly sold for local consumption. Now it's promoting *vi novell*, bringing young wines to the market about six weeks after harvest. The Ampurdán region also produces sparkling wines by both large container and champagne methods. Very popular is Blanc Pescador, a light, frisky *pétillant* wine (slightly sparkling), which is a good companion to seafood. Many restaurants will have a *vino de la casa*, house wine. Regional restaurants will feature wines from their region in Catalunya or another parts of Spain. Many will have a selection from Rioja, Spain's best-known wine region. See what local people are drinking or ask the waiter for advice. See **Drinks**.